IMAGES *of our Past*

HISTORIC
DIGBY

MIKE PARKER

NIMBUS
PUBLISHING

Nimbus Publishing Limited
PO Box 9166
Halifax, NS   B3K 5M8
(902) 455-4286
www.nimbus.ns.ca

Design: Joan Sinclair

Printed and bound in Canada

Canadian Cataloguing in Publication Data

Parker, Mike, 1952-

      Historic Digby
      Includes bibliographical references.
      ISBN 1-55109-339-1

1. Digby (N.S.) — History.   2. Digby (N.S. : County) — History.   I. Title.
FC2345.D53P37 2000   971.6'32   C00-950194-0
F1039.D5P37 2000

Front cover:

DIGBY SCALLOPS

The Pines Hotel backdrops this c. 1930 photo of an early scallop boat and three-masted schooner moored dockside at the Racquette. See page 48.

Title page:

POST CARD VIEW OF DIGBY GUT, CA 1930.

"Annapolis Basin, outlet of the River of that name, is a beautiful, placid sheet of water, extending from the mouth of Bear River to the remarkable strait called by the Aborigines "Tee-wee-den," signifying "Little Hole," by the English, "St. George's Channel," but now known as Annapolis and Digby Gut; being a narrow gap in the North Mountain one half mile wide, with trappean cliffs rising on either side to a great height, and through which Strait the tides of both Annapolis Basin and the Bay of Fundy rush very rapidly."

Canada   The Canada Council | Le Conseil des Arts
              for the Arts | du Canada

Nimbus Publishing acknowledges financial support for our publishing activities from the Government of Canada through the Book Publishing Industry Development Program (BPIDP), and the Canada Council.

Dedication

For my mom, Geraldine Parker, 1916-1975

Acknowledgements

My thanks to Taunya Dawson and all the volunteers at the Admiral Digby Museum, Gary Shutlak at the Public Archives of Nova Scotia, Lynn-Marie Richard at the Maritime Museum of the Atlantic, Ralph Getson at the Fisheries Museum of the Atlantic, Archer Turnbull, Louise Morse Warne, Maxine Connell, Francis Adams, Lance Woolaver, and Graham McBride. A special debt of gratitude goes to Norman Wright, whose untiring work and wit were indispensable and greatly appreciated.

Contents

Introduction

The history of Digby, it has been said, "is not one of cruel wars and bloody battles, but rather a story of the successful efforts of a group of pioneers to carve out of the wilderness a home where they could continue in their loyalty to King as well as country. It is the story of families who faced hardship and privation rather than accept a concept of patriotism which denied allegiances they felt they could not abandon."

The American Revolutionary War of 1775-83 pitted Whig supporters of independence against Tory compatriots—known as United Empire Loyalists—who maintained allegiance to British sovereignty. Isaiah Wilson writes in his Digby County history that "the latter did not, as a rule, uphold the King or Parliament in their attempts to tax the Colonies, but they thought that whatever evils existed through Legislation in England could be cured by Constitutional methods without recourse to rebellion, and they maintained they had a right to freedom of opinion on this point; and further that they ought not to be coerced into an attitude of hostility against the Government of England." As the colonial war progressively moved in favour of the revolutionists, a small Loyalist delegation led by Amos Botsford left New York in 1782 on a "colonizing mission" to Nova Scotia. After visiting Annapolis, Conway (Digby) and Parr Town (Saint John), reports submitted in January 1783 stated that, because of its rich soil and fishery, "some of our people choose Conway." Comparisons were made to the Annapolis Basin, St. Mary's Bay, and the St. John River as being "equal" to the Connecticut and Hudson Rivers.

Soliciting Agent Botsford cautioned at the time that "Conway will have to go through a regular Process in the Court of Escheats, having already been granted." This was in reference to a hundred-thousand-acre grant issued in 1765 to Alexander McNutt & Associates from Ulster, Ireland, who had plans for settling Irish emigrants on lands that would later com-

ALONE AT THE WHEEL

LEFT

A 1911 Frederick William Wallace photo of an unidentified crewman at the wheel of the Digby fishing schooner Dorothy G. Snow. *"When it is really cold at sea, it's cruelly cold and penetrating," Wallace wrote of winter fishing. "Fingers and toes were numb within a very brief time as the insidious frost crept in. Oilskins became stiff as tin. The eyes, watering in the wind and with staring into the binnacle, froze their lashes together." Frederick William Wallace's numerous books documenting Canada's sailing-ship history and early fishing industry development are considered definitive works. Of particular interest to the Digby story is the* Roving Fisherman, *which recounts in graphic detail Wallace's first-hand experiences sailing aboard Digby fishing schooners, the stark reality of a fisherman's life in the days of sail, and the unfailing faith Digby crews placed in the wooden vessels that took them to sea.*

prise the Loyalist Townships of Digby and Weymouth. Stretching from Joggin to the Sissiboo River, the proposed township had been named Conway in honour of General Henry Seymour Conway, Commander-in-Chief of the British Army. A condition of the grant was that 50 families, each to receive five hundred acres, be settled in Conway within a year or the lands would be liable to forfeit. McNutt had failed to satisfy these terms, and much of the grant remained vacant when Botsford arrived—with the exception of about a hundred pre-Loyalists, primarily New England fishermen who had settled in the 1760s near future Loyalist sites such as Digby, Weymouth, Freeport, and Westport. A Notice for Escheat of Conway Grant was posted in Halifax on March 17, 1783 but never prosecuted. Failure to do so would later result in years of litigation over conflicting land titlement claims.

On June 1, 1783 the *Atalanta*, a 14-gun sloop under the command of Robert Digby, Rear Admiral of the British Fleet, arrived at Conway from New York with the first detachment of United Empire Loyalists. Work began immediately on building temporary shelters along the west shore of Annapolis Basin "on the pleasant slope of a declivity facing the rising sun." Within days the transports *Union, Peggy, Sally, King George, Bridgewater* and *Townsend* sailed into the basin with additional settlers. "Determined to advance, the emigrants resolved to erect a Town at their new abode, hoping it would become a large and opulent City." Deputy Surveyor Thomas Milledge laid out a 70-acre town plot, which included nine North and South directional streets (Water, Queen, King, West, Cemetery, First, Second, Third, Fourth Avenues) and eight intersecting cross streets (Carleton, Prince William, Sydney, Church, Mount, Warwick, St. Mary's Bay and George). Three diagonal streets, necessitated by the curvature of land along the shoreline, were named Birch Place, Maiden Lane, and Montague Row.

A late arrival at Conway was the ship *Joseph* owned by New York merchants Rutherford and Nash. Sailing from New York on October 18, 1783 the *Joseph* eventually reached Long Island, Digby County after a two month storm-battered voyage; from here, Nathaniel Bates piloted the transport to its destination. Wilson gives an entertaining account of the ship's passage through Digby Gut:

> "A record kept by one of the emigrants, states that when approaching the entrance, many on board becoming alarmed at the narrowness of the passage, feared the craft could not pass the barrier. Great consternation and dread dismay pervaded their minds on that memorable tenth of December. Females wrung their hands and screamed frantically, expecting every moment the frail bark would be dashed in pieces by the high cliffs rising in sublime grandeur on either side. Unable to allay their fears, and having no other recourse, they were ordered into the hold, and the hatches promptly closed. Several

sailors also refused duty for a time, confident further advancement was impossible. However, the brave, expert Pilot, accustomed to the Channel, steered his charge safely to anchor in the beautiful Basin."

With winter at hand, most chose to remain within the confines of cramped ship's quarters until spring, although a few families landed on Christmas Day and built crude camps along the shore. Despite the many hardships of the next few months, "the genial society on board and in the settlement excited high hopes, and intensified firm resolves to fully improve the coming summer in preparations, appropriate and ample, for enjoying succeeding years."

In 1783, Digby comprised "a full Colony of true and noble Patriots" hailing predominately from New York and New Jersey. "Many of the settlers had passed middle life before reaching Nova Scotia. But the larger number still possessed their full strength and had marvellous powers of endurance." There were merchants, tradesmen, farmers, physicians, fishermen, disbanded soldiers, and "some gentlemen of great emminence in wealth and high attainments." One noteworthy name among them was John Edison, great-grandfather of the inventor Thomas Alva Edison. Listing nine in the family on the 1783 muster role, the Edisons are believed to have lived on a farm in Marshalltown from 1790-1811, and to have owned large tracts of land in North and South Range, as well as several lots in Digby. John Edison was director of the town marsh from 1799-1808, and also served as an assessor of the poor. His eldest son Samuel (Thomas Edison's grandfather) was 14 when the family moved from New Jersey, and eventually succeeded his father as marsh overseer in 1808. Samuel Edison Jr. (Thomas Edison's father) was born in Digby on August 6, 1803. Shortly after, and for unknown reasons, the Edisons packed up in 1811 and moved to the Township of Bayhem in the District of London, Ontario.

It has been said that the Edison family had a "proclivity for involvement in rebellion"—a fact borne out by Samuel Jr., who fled to the United States in 1837 after fighting for William Lyon MacKenzie in the failed Upper Canada Rebellion of 1837-38. Before him, his father had held the rank of Captain in the 1812 War, while patriarch John Edison fought on the British side during the colonial war—in opposition to his own father Thomas, who backed the revolutionists. Thomas Alva Edison (1847-1931) was born in Ohio and listed among his many inventions are the light bulb, telephone transmitter, phonograph, motion-picture equipment, stock ticker, and mimeograph machine. His son Charles (1890-1969) became a prominent American politician, rising to the post of Secretary of the Navy, then Governor of New Jersey in 1941, the same state that, in 1783, his great-great-grandfather had fled.

Within a year of settlement, Conway's muster role listed 1,295 names, with more than two hundred new homes. A number of Loyalists brought oak house frames with them; according to Isaiah Wilson, "these were speedily erected on grounds hastily cleared by the willing and determined band, who laboured constantly throughout the season in clearing the forests and securing their families and effects from the elements. Many built houses of logs, corked with moss, until more commodious edifices could be reared. Several of these, afterwards enlarged, covered with boards and shingles, stood over one hundred years...." The King's Bounty provided three years' worth of provisions—including boards, bricks and nails—to those who qualified. Records indicate that only 24 people were refused assistance. A 1784 report submitted by John Robinson (whose duty it was to enumerate those persons "soliciting provisions as they were suffering for want of life's necessaries"), made special note of the fact that Digby Loyalists were "extremely industrious, and have exerted themselves to the utmost of their abilities in improving the settlement, by which means it is already in a flourishing condition; and it is probable, from the goodness of the Harbour, and its advantageous situation, it will become a place of consequence." In 1787, at the settlers' request, government replaced "Conway" on the new Botsford grant with "Digby," to honour the Admiral whose charge it had been to oversee their safe conveyance and settlement. Rear Admiral Robert Digby (1732-1815) took an active interest in the town's advancement, building a home on Maiden Lane, to which he returned on several occasions, and contributing to the establishment of Trinity Anglican Church.

Digby was not the only "place of consequence" in 1783-84, as increasing numbers of Loyalists settled at Weymouth, St. Mary's Bay (Brighton and Barton), Brier and Long Islands, and along Digby Neck in such communities as Sandy Cove, Little River, and Gullivers Cove.

"Notwithstanding their hardships, tradition says they appeared as happy as 'Parsons Pig,' having their chopping frolics by day, and winding up with a dance in the evening."

The first town in what eventually comprised Digby County was settled five months before Admiral Digby's transports arrived at Conway. Anthony Stewart and Samuel Gouldsbury, Scotsmen from New York, explored St. Mary's Bay and, on January 21, 1783, landed settlers on the west side of Sissiboo River at "Gouldsbury's Point." Few details exist of this settlement (named "New Edinburgh") other than the fact that Anthony Stewart— "chief promotor of the enterprise"—had been imprisoned at New York and forfeited his possessions for being a Tory sympathizer during the war. New Edinburgh's time was relatively short, as a number of its people became discouraged and left to live with relatives or friends at newly-settled Shelburne and Saint John. Others moved across the Sissiboo and took up residency along various points of the river in the soon-to-be Loyalist town of Weymouth. One of the foremost names listed in the New Edinburgh patent was Reverend Charles Inglis, who later moved to Halifax where, in 1787, he was consecrated the first Bishop of Nova Scotia. By the late 1800s only a few overgrown streets remained as testament to the original New

Captain John Beaman & Family

The muster roll of 1784 listed three Beamans among its civilian numbers: Ebenezer Beaman, Thomas Beaman (a merchant), and widow Elizabeth Beaman. In April 1801, a Joseph Beaman, along with Joseph Titus, supervised the building of a fishing weir at the Racquette. Beamans must have played a significant role in Digby's history, as Ben Lomond Mountain to the north of town was at some point renamed Beaman's Mountain. Little is known about Captain John Beaman, seen here with wife Lavenia Sophia and their four children in a stoic pose typical of early portrait photography. His parents, Mr. and Mrs. David Beaman of Digby, had six children—three sons and three daughters. John and Edward lived in Digby and George in Saint John, N.B. Two daughters married—Mrs. Henry Haines of Lynn and Mrs. S.E. Logan of Saint John—while the third, Miss Emma Beaman, "a highly respected resident of Digby," died a spinster.

Captain John Beaman's wife Lavenia Sophia (1845-1927) was born in Digby (Lavenia was descended from French Huguenot Jean Aymar, who emigrated to New York from France); their children's names were Harry, Elizabeth, and Georgie; a third unknown daughter married a Dr. D. Moore. Miss Georgie Beaman lost her bakery business in the Digby Fire of 1899. Captain John Beaman no doubt sailed during the era of Digby's wooden ships. In his later years, Beaman was a prominent member of the Western Nova Scotia Yacht Club, skippering the yacht Dorothy, *"one of the fastest in the Club," to a number of first place finishes.*

Edinburgh townsite, the area having become populated "by a goodly number of farm houses peopled by English and Acadiens." The failure of some Loyalists to tough it out in the early stages of settlement was common, particularly among the wealthy, who had the financial means to leave after experiencing conditions to which they were unaccustomed. It's estimated that 90 "white Loyalist" families and 34 "of African descent" left the Digby area between the years 1785 and 1798. However, a healthy birth rate, combined with an influx of Scottish Crofters in 1789, more than compensated for such losses.

Blacks figured prominently in Digby's early years. More than thirty thousand Loyalists emigrated to Nova Scotia in the 1780s, and about 10 percent of these were free Blacks. The 211 who settled on the outskirts of Digby at Brindley Town were the second largest number in Nova Scotia. Brindley Town, Birchtown, and Little Tracadie were the only all-Black settlements in the province. Of the 48 communities considered historically significant today in Nova Scotia's Black history, eight are in Digby County: Acaciaville, Conway, Jordantown, Digby, Weymouth, Southville, Haslett, and Danver. The noted Reverend Richard Preston—who escaped slavery in 1816 and came to Nova Scotia—founded the Acaciaville United Baptist Church in 1853. A year later this was one of 12 churches organized by Reverend Preston into the African United Baptist Association, considered "the key institution of Black Nova Scotia life."

Two other peoples who factored in the Digby story are Mi'kmaq and French Acadiens. By the time of Loyalist settlement, the once-warring Mi'kmaq—who sided with the French in their battle for Acadia—had been at peace with Britain for 20 years. The subsequent fate of native peoples from the ravages of disease and at the hands of colonial authorities has been well documented. Mi'kmaq living in Digby County tended to congregate at Bear River, Digby Gut, and the Acadien district of Clare where they maintained summer coastal fishing camps along St. Mary's Bay. Increasingly pressed for traditional territories by non-native encroachment, Mi'kmaq were pushed toward reserve life in the early 1800s. At Bear River in 1820, one thousand acres were established as a government reserve, though it was not until around 1828 that several families moved onto the lands, under Chief Andrew Meuse. Although limited educational opportunities were available on the Bear River reserve, the 1872 building of a federally-funded school was the first of its kind in Atlantic Canada. Of the approximately 1,700 Mi'kmaq living in Nova Scotia c. 1871, the counties of Digby (with 224) and neighbouring Annapolis (with 63) had the largest concentration of Mi'kmaq in the province.

Digby's French connection dates to 1604-1605, when DeMonts and Champlain detailed their explorations of the Bay of Fundy, St. Mary's Bay, and the Annapolis Basin, prior to settling at Port Royal. They were followed to "La Cadie" by large numbers of French emigrants in the seventeenth century, who settled predominantly along marshlands of the Annapolis River and Minas Basin. When more than seven thousand Acadiens were expelled in 1755 for refusing to swear allegiance to the British crown, some of those who escaped to the woods in advance of Winslow's troops were drawn to the salt marshes and fisheries of St. Mary's Bay. Most would have starved had they not been cared for by their long-time Mi'kmaq allies. "Plain and unassuming in their dress and manners, they have ever overcome almost insurmountable difficulties with surprising success and adroitness." With repatriation in 1764, with the granting of Clare township along St. Mary's Bay in 1767, and with the willingness of many exiled Acadiens to endure, in 1768, an 825-mile return journey on foot, a vibrant French presence took hold in Digby County.

The naming of Nova Scotia's Clare reportedly has an Irish connection. In 1276, Thomas de Clare was granted a district on the west coast of Ireland by his friend Edward I of England. Originally known as "Thomond," the district was later changed to "Clare" in recognition of its owner. Michael Franklyn, Lieutenant-Governor of Nova Scotia in 1767, apparently saw fit to name the new Acadien township along the west shore of St. Mary's Bay after Thomas de Clare, who was himself of French extraction.

Records indicate that a Mrs. Charles Marien Belliveau at Presque Isle, Church Point "felled the first large tree cut by the newcomers in Clare." Digby County's first burial ground was located on Major's Point at the Acadien community of Belliveau Cove, and the *premier* Acadien born in newly-established Clare was a boy, Joseph, who arrived on September 25, 1768 to parents Marie Robichaud and Joseph Dugas. Better known today as the French Shore, the Municipality of Clare has been called the "Longest Main Street in the World." Stretching 40 km from St. Bernard to Salmon River, "a succession of Acadien villages border each other so closely it is difficult to determine, except by road signs, where one ends and the other begins." Two of its dominant landmarks are St. Mary's Church, at Church Point, and St. Bernard Church, at Belliveau Cove. St. Mary's was built between 1903 and 1905 and is the largest wooden church in Canada, its two-hundred-foot spire anchored at the base by 36 tons of concrete to control sway. Also at Pointe de l'Église is l'Université Sainte-Anne, founded in the early 1890s by Eudist priests. The magnificent St. Bernard stone edifice, which seats a thousand, was erected one row a year between 1910 and 1942, its granite blocks carried by train and ox team 120 miles from Shelburne, then cut to shape by local artisans. Today the Municipality of Clare within the County of Digby has 9,600 inhabitants, the largest Acadien population in Nova Scotia.

Digby was spared the pillage and plunder of the earlier wars inflicted on the neighbouring settlement of Annapolis Royal. Two years before Digby's founding, American "rebel" schooners had sacked Annapolis, and in 1782 the *Atalanta* was deployed in the Bay of Fundy to drive away pirate intruders. During the Napoleonic and 1812 Wars, French and Yankee privateers continually threatened but never attacked Digby, "occasioning great anxiety." One notable incident happened on July 31, 1812 when a privateer anchored between Broad Cove and Roger's Point, only a short distance from Digby. A militia unit "marched thither, attacked the unwelcome visitor, fired over fifty shots into her, receiving some in return and obliged the intruder to leave our shore." Another occasion recounted in Wilson's history involved a Captain William Taylor from Digby, who built the schooner *Hairm* "for returning those unkindly compliments from the belligerent country. Though hastily constructed, she soon taught the 'Sons of Freedom' that Digby was fully determined and also amply able to be free indeed."

With the conclusion of hostilities in 1815, Digby could finally relax its vigilance and get on with forging a thriving existence. Lumbering and fishing became the trademark industries, with farming playing an important but secondary role. By the late 1800s, Bear River and Weymouth were the acknowledged lumbering centres of the county, with Bear River's wood and lumber trade totalling $85,000 a year, and with Weymouth's exports of more than 12 million feet of lumber (plus cordwood and piling) valued at $145,000 annually. An additional eight million feet of lumber were shipped from ports stretching from Salmon River to the head of St. Mary's Bay.

For the fishery, Boutilier and Morehouse at Centreville on Digby Neck were said to have "premises the largest probably of any in the county." Established in the 1880s, the company employed 30 workers in a factory that produced, each year, seventy-two thousand cans of finnan haddies and lobsters, in addition to dry and boneless fish and fish oil. "The two members of the firm," according to an 1897 *Digby Weekly Courier,* "are wide-awake men who work on principles of down-deep honesty in every branch of their business....In every sense, Boutilier & Morehouse are one of the leading firms engaged in the Nova Scotia fish trade and are enjoying a reputation which comes from merit."

Early on, Digby was designated a Port of Entry attached to Shelburne, with Loyalist James Wilmot appointed the first Collector and Deputy Registrar of Deeds and Conveyances. Domestic and foreign trade increased, with a corresponding growth in shipbuilding. Sail and steam-driven packets carried mail, produce, and passengers between Saint John, Digby, and Annapolis. Schooners and square riggers plied the American eastern seaboard to the West Indies and crossed the Atlantic to Great Britain. The coming of the railway in 1879—as well as steadily-improved steamship service to Saint John, and interconnecting lines from Boston and New York—all enhanced Digby's popularity as a summer retreat for the burgeoning American tourist trade of the late nineteenth century. The railway and steamship also gave Digby an inside track on competitors in the development of its fresh fishery, which in the early 1900s became more popular with consumers than traditional salted and dried varieties. A boast in 1914 was that Canadian Pacific Railway could land fish in Montreal a mere 18 hours after it made dockside in Digby. "It is quite frequently the case in preparing rush shipments of fresh fish to have them thrown out of the boats between the hours of dawn and noon, almost flapping, packed and on board the steamship by 1:30, in St. John by 4:45 and in Montreal next morning at eight o'clock."

A few points need be made regarding nineteenth-century Digby's civic and political development. As mentioned earlier, a Notice for Escheat of Conway Grant, at the recommendation of Amos Botsford was posted in Halifax on March 17, 1783, prior to Admiral Digby's arrival. Many years passed before people demanded some form of action to settle the land title once and for all. In 1795 a "Bill to Quiet the Possession of Land within the Township of Digby" was introduced to the House of Assembly in Halifax. Judgement was delayed for another six years, until the contentious Conway and Botsford Grants issue was at last settled on January 29, 1801, with the proclamation of the Hatfield Grant, known also as the the Grant of Confirmation. Affecting 275 individuals and one church, "the proclamation of this grant enabled those who had made improvements on lands they already occupied to obtain legal title and therefore sell or mortgage their property as they saw fit."

The five provincial counties of Annapolis, Queens, Lunenburg, Halifax, and Kings were established in 1759. Digby remained a part of Annapolis County until April 21, 1837 when a division of Annapolis formed the new County of Digby comprising the Townships of Digby and Clare, Bear Island, Long Island, Brier Island and "that part of the Township of Clements lying to the Westward of Bear River." On March 29, 1838 the Township of Clements, then in Digby County, was renamed the Township of Hillsburgh, and Digby was designated the County or Shire Town. On April 10, 1841 Weymouth became a separate Township. When the Municipalities of Digby and Clare, to be governed by their own officers, were established on November 18, 1879, Digby Municipality comprised the old townships of Hillsburgh, Digby, Weymouth, and Westport. Provincial Secretary W.S. Fielding granted the incorporation of Digby as a town on February 28, 1890; Thomas C. Shreve, Q.C., was voted Digby's first mayor, with elected councillors Orbin Sproul, Sydney Wood, Henry G. Turnbull, Thomas Boyne, Edmund Biden, and John Daley.

Digby town and county are connected to several noteworthy events that are beyond the scope of this book but still deserve mention.

THE NOVA SCOTIA PONY EXPRESS

This short-lived but exciting venture is described in a 1912 paper by John W. Regan for the Nova Scotia Historical Society:

> "The Associated Press, the greatest news-gathering organization in existence, had its inception in a 'pony express' started by six New York newspapers, that was operated between Halifax and Digby in 1849,

for the purpose of forwarding European news to Boston and New York in advance of the arrival at Boston of the English mail steamer from Halifax. The 'pony express' terminated at Victoria Beach near Digby, where a chartered steamboat was waiting to convey the dispatches across the Bay of Fundy to Saint John, the terminus of the newly-constructed electric telegraph line, and from this point the news was wired to New York, many hours [36] ahead of the arrival of the English mail steamers from Liverpool and Halifax."

The Pony Express route followed the Old Post Road from Halifax to Victoria Beach (on the eastern shore of Annapolis Basin, near Digby Gut). Its termination point was technically within Annapolis County, but Digby was only a gunshot across the water from Victoria Beach, and would have been abuzz with excitement. The distance between points of 144 miles was covered in an average time of 8 hours, using a relay of 12 horses and 2 riders, who exchanged dispatches at Kentville. For a short time there were apparently two rival factions backing separate pony expresses: the Associated Press, and a consortium of New York businessmen and speculators. One race to Victoria Beach—involving 4 riders and 24 horses—ended with the Associated Press rider arriving a mere two-and-a-half minutes in the lead. The Nova Scotia Pony Express began in February of 1849 and ended only nine months later, when the telegraph was extended from Saint John to Sackville, N.B. and then to Halifax.

MURDER AND MAYHEM

Two Digby vessels have links with high seas mystery and murder. On November 7, 1872 the 103-foot brigantine *Mary Celeste* sailed from New York for Genoa, Italy. One month later she was found floating, abandoned, 590 miles west of Gibraltar by the Digby brigantine *Dei Gratia*. All her cargo and personal effects were intact, with no apparent sign of struggle or storm damage. Despite many theories, no concrete evidence was ever produced as to the fate of crew and passengers.

There was plenty of detail, however, about the gruesome mutiny aboard another Digby ship. In 1871, the 984-ton *Lennie* was built at Belliveau Cove for W.D. Lovitt and Smith Horton of Yarmouth. Four years later this vessel was involved in one of the world's most famous mutinies. On October 23, 1875, the *Lennie* left Antwerp for Sandy Hook with Stanley Hatfield of Yarmouth as Captain and Richard McDonald of Saint John as Second Mate. The 11-man crew was a melting pot of nationalities. Only days out of the English Channel, an unexplained revolt resulted in both Captain Hatfield and Second-Mate McDonald being stabbed to death and thrown overboard. The mutineers, none of whom could navigate, were tricked by a Belgian, Van Hoydonck, into thinking they had set course for Gibraltar, when in reality the vessel was headed into the Bristol Channel. When suspicions arose, Van Hoydonck altered course several times over the next few days, throwing bottles containing scribbled pleas for help overboard and eventually being rescued by a French gunboat. The subsequent trial resulted in the execution of four mutineers, and in Van Hoydonck's decoration by four governments; he was also compensated handsomely for salvage rights by the *Lennie*'s owners.

ON THE MARCH: THE NORTH WEST MOUNTED POLICE

Freeport, Long Island native Samuel Thurber was honoured in November 1999 at a 125th commemorative ceremony, held in the community by members of the Royal Canadian Mounted Police. The occasion marked Thurber's westward march in 1874 as an original member of the North West Mounted Police. Born on November 30, 1844, Thurber worked in his early years as a fisherman and farmer. In 1873 the North-West Mounted Police was formed—mainly as a response to the Manitoba Cypress Hills massacre in May of that year, when a dispute between wolf hunters and Assiniboine Indians resulted in the killing of women and children. It is reported that 29-year-old Samuel Thurber "fell in with Captain Carvell who was recruiting moral men of good character to join a troop to go out to Manitoba as mounted police." Thurber signed up at Halifax, was assigned regimental number 87, and ended up at Lower Fort Gary where he was sworn in. Then began the four month trek westward: 275 men covering 12-14 miles a day, enduring oppressive heat, mosquitos, grasshoppers, snow, and hail the size of walnuts, and losing 60 horses in the ordeal. After serving a western tour of duty from 1873-1876, Thurber left the NWMP and returned to Freeport; he went to sea for the remainder of his days, travelling the globe and eventually captaining his own vessel. He is buried in Freeport's Valley Cemetery, where a cairn was erected in 1973 to mark the RCMP's one hundredth anniversary.

"WHITE-WASHED YANKEES"

It was common in the late 1800s for Nova Scotia fishermen to leave their native province and head for Gloucester, Massachusetts, where opportunities of higher wages beckoned. One of these "white-washed Yankees" (as they came to be known) was Digby's Marty Welch (c.1867-1935), who sailed 40 years aboard American vessels. Only 14 when he started, it has been written of Captain Welch that "No college of learning opened its doors...Marty's college was a dory—the bow of it—and his diploma an oar with which to earn his living." Welch honed his skills under the tutelage of noted vessel designer T.F. McManus and legendary Gloucester skippers Eben Lewis and Maurice Whalen, later captaining several U.S. schooners himself while building a reputation as a "killer" in the mackerel and haddock fishery. His greatest claim to fame was as skipper of the schooner *Esperanto*, which defeated the Canadian entry *Delawana* in 1920 to give the Americans the Halifax Herald Trophy in the inaugural North Atlantic Fishermen's International Race. Marty Welch was at the helm of *Elsie* the following year when Lunenburg's Captain Angus Walters and *Bluenose* won back the championship mantle. Upon his death in 1935, Captain Marty Welch was acclaimed as "one of the greatest sailing masters out of Gloucester."

HUNGRY FOR HISTORY

Isaiah Woodworth Wilson was born on March 8, 1848 at Hill Grove, Digby County. Described in his later years as a "little whiskered, near-sighted man" Wilson travelled the county on foot for more than half a century, selling *Belcher's Almanacs* and helping organize Sons of Temperance Lodges wherever he went. Possessing a keen memory and, from a young age, a penchant for Digby's history, Wilson began, in 1867, to preserve the story of his native county, combining facts gathered from frequent sojourns among village residents with his own painstaking archival research— a 26-year quest. Combing the Records Office in Weymouth and the *Digby Courier* files, Wilson also walked to Halifax and back, on more than one occasion, to gather information from the N.S. Legislative Library. His efforts finally came to fruitation in 1893, when *A Geography & History of the County of Digby* was published in Halifax. Unfortunately, Wilson didn't have the financial means to purchase his book for re-sale and it languished at the publishers until 1917, when William Snow from Smith's Cove brokered a deal to buy the books at a discount, then sold them to Wilson, who peddled his life's work door to door. Isaiah Wilson died in October 1928 but his legacy lives on. Limited copies of *A Geography & History of the County of Digby* were republished in 1999 by the Admiral Digby Museum.

There is a saying that the more things change, the more they stay the same. Such is the case with Digby. Certainly societal values, daily life, and the workplace are far different than those of Isaiah Wilson's day, but striking similarties link the present Digby to its past. Digby's forests and fishery, for example, still figure in many of its people's livelihoods. The county's population has remained virtually unchanged for a century, the census of 1891 listing 19,983; that of 1991 showing 21,250. Resident numbers in Digby town have consistently remained at around two thousand since the early 1900s (Statistics Canada figures for 1951 report 2,047; increasing in 1981 to a high of 2,558; then dropping again in 1996 to 2,199). The recent decline in population is no doubt attributable to the demise of the Atlantic fishery. "Life in Nova Scotia fishing ports is an adjustment to a brutal new reality," writes Rob Gorham in the November 26, 1997 *Halifax Chronicle-Herald*. "The resource that once made them rich has collapsed and they must diversify to survive. Across Nova Scotia, fishing communities are facing this dilemma with varying degrees of success." The inshore scallop industry and lobster fishery "remain key components" of Digby's present economy. In 1997 its one hundred scallop boats were said to comprise 90 percent of Nova Scotia's inshore scallop fleet.

With the dramatic downturn in the ground fishery, Digby's links with its past once more come to the forefront with the renewed emphasis on maximizing its tourist potential. A summer-vacation mecca a hundred years ago, Digby town and county have experienced a renaissance of late, being recognized in several regional and national magazines as one of the most "romantic" spots in Canada. Recent developments along Digby's waterfront include a boardwalk and marina, bus tours abound, and cruise ship business is actively sought by the Port of Digby Cruise Ship Association. The Islands and Digby Neck Community Development Associations have plans for a 60-kilometre hiking trail from Point Prim (near Digby) to Western Light on Brier Island, a trail that will eventually connect with the Trans-Canada Trail, scheduled to pass through Digby. Many county outports offer eco-tourism adventures that focus on whale and bird watching, and on the natural surrounding splendour. The Municipality of Clare takes pride in showcasing its Acadian culture, and will be front and centre in 2004 when Nova Scotia hosts the third World Acadian Congress.

Digby has long taken a backseat to other towns and counties in Nova Scotia, in terms of its popular history. This is unfortunate since it sits at the doorstep of Port Royal, Canada's birthplace. History is the sum of its parts, and the story of Digby is one such crucial piece. To this end, an inventory of heritage buildings in the county has recently been undertaken, and several historical societies operate museum interpretative programs. Isaiah Wilson was the first to recognize the importance of preserving Digby's storied past; he was followed in later years by the writings of Reverend Allan Massie Hill, Reverend Walter R. Greenwood, Hazel M. Clayton, R. Baden Powell, and Victor G. Cardoza. *Historic Digby* is meant to be a companion to these earlier works. No book of this nature can do justice to more than two centuries of history. The intent, here, is to provide a pictorial vignette, highlighting the years around the late nineteenth and early twentieth century. In the words of Marcus Garvey, the prolific American Black historian—"a people without knowledge of their history is like a tree without roots." It is hoped that *Historic Digby* will foster both knowledge and pride—and perhaps an interest in discovering more about Digby's heritage as it enters a new millenium.

WATER STREET, DIGBY, 1890

Chapter 1

Streetscapes of Digby

THE CHERRY TREE STAND

Conveniently located near a thoroughfare from the Dominion Atlantic Railway Station on First Avenue and Government Wharf, the Cherry Tree Stand at the corner of Prince William and Birch Streets was a favourite stop for ice-cream. George Winfield is said to have operated this summer canteen in the west corner of his mother's tourist home, Winfield Lodge, in the early 1900s. An 1897 *Illustrated Summer Digby Courier* edition made special note of an earlier ice cream vendor: "The necessaries of a summer existence include nowadays the erstwhile luxuries of ice-cream and fruit. The sedative influences of these edibles, as furnished by G.H. Holdsworth, combine with natural beauties and charms to make a stay in Digby enjoyable. In other words the best ice-cream in town is Holdworth's. His parlors are fitted up with every convenience and neatness and are the favourite resort of tourist and residents alike."

CANNON BANKS, C. 1890

From the arrival of Loyalist settlers in 1783, writes county historian Isaiah Wilson, "no special events marked the Military phase from close of the War of 1783, to the Contest between France and Britain ten years later. Evidently the Government considered Digby almost impregnable without fortifications, as no sufficient protective implements or structures had yet been supplied. But when war was imminent, the state of her defences received early attention." Physical evidence suggests there had been some type of British fortifications at Digby Gut prior to 1781 but these had disappeared by the time of settlement.

In 1794, the Queen's Battery was built on the Cannon Banks, a parcel of land at the north end of town later known as Robinson's Point. Comprised of a small blockhouse, ditch, drawbridge, and outer parapet with five cannons, erosion destroyed much of the original battery by 1856. At the time of this late-nineteenth-century photo, only the ordinance remained as testament to Digby's earlier days. The beached three-masted schooner was the *John*, a Norwegian wreck that was eventually burned to salvage her copper fastenings.

BLOCK HOUSE C. 1870

A rare photo of the block house erected in 1813 above Water Street in Second Division J, between King and Queen Streets. Two others were built during the 1812 War along St. George's Channel at the entrance to Digby Gut. The larger Duke of York's Battery was strategically positioned on the eastern approaches near Victoria Beach, while Prince Regent's Battery, "also respectable, having four guns," protected the Digby shore from a 50-foot elevation on the cliffs, near to where the life-saving station sits today. A fourth small battery was located at Racquette Point. A Regiment of Militia Volunteers, comprised of ten companies, was organized in 1793 to defend Digby, Annapolis Royal, and St. Mary's Bay from "surprises on the surrounding country" by roving privateers in the Bay of Fundy. Digby's defenses were scaled back following the cessation of hostilities in 1815, although a small detachment from the Annapolis Royal garrison continued to man Prince Regent's Battery until 1820.

WATER STREET, C. 1890

Water Street was the heart of Digby's commercial district. Facing south on the right is the dormered three-storey Royal Hotel, owned by John Daley. A barber's pole and Hardy Bent's shoeshine kiosk are also visible. Across the street near the buckboard is a vendor's sign advertising 'Soda Water.' Henry Rutherford and George Nash were Digby's first merchants, opening Rutherford & Nash in 1784—a "General Store on the Retail principle." This was actually the continuation of a shipping and mercantile partnership that the two men had established in 1772 at White Plains, New Jersey. Other businessmen listed among the founding Loyalists were Gilbert and Jonathan Fowler as 'Fowler Bros,' John Hill, John Smith, Robert

Ray, Joseph Fitzrandolph, James Crowley, Thomas Beaman and William McDonnell. Robert Ray operated the first liquor establishment. James D. Holdsworth later opened a 'liquor store' on his lot at the junction of Water Street and Montague Row. "Liquor venders were always numerous. All the oldest tradesmen were licensed for this purpose. Hence they were sold in same buildings with other merchandize." Some early Digby craftsmen were coopers Thomas Ellis, Abraham Miller, and John Thompson; blacksmiths Jacob Dakin, Sr. and Isaac Roop; tailors James Richards and Conrad Handlespiker; Dougald McCassell, weaver; Joshua Smith, tanner; Henry Snelling, jeweller; Isaac Longsworth and John C. Small, boot and shoe manufacturers.

'Bummers Crossing'

A buckboard bumps along over railroad tracks in this late 1890s photo taken at the intersection of Water and Birch Streets, where Water veers right leading down to the Government Wharf. The commercial building with a flag pole in the foreground is thought to have been built in 1874 by Joseph S. Cutten of Truro, a contractor with the Western Counties Railway, which had plans of building a line from Yarmouth to Annapolis Royal. Railway tracks were only inches from the front of this building because the spur line to the wharf was not built until c. 1895 when available space was at a premium. The two-storey structure to the rear was the original Waverly House, a tourist establishment owned by a Miss Forsythe and Mrs. Joseph Merritt; it was destroyed in the fire of 1899.

This busy area of town at the tracks was known as 'Bummers Crossing,' a place frequented by the less fortunate seeking handouts from passersby. There was always something of interest to see on nineteenth century Water Street. The volunteer militia often marched through town—led by lone bandsman Mr. Donegan on the clarinet—on its way to or from training exercises on the Cannon Banks. 'Old Sevastopol,' an aged veteran of the Crimean War, was a common sight walking along the street and into shops, with advertising billboards draped from his back. Another old-timer by the name of Daddy Andrews daily searched both sides of Water Street, with two wooden shingles, for the ever-plentiful manure heaps to "replenish his fertilizer pile."

DIGBY FIRE OF 1899

Disaster struck Digby on Monday, February 13, 1899 when fire razed a large portion of the downtown commercial district. Originating in the furnace room of G.I Letteney and Bro's store on Water Street, flames were first detected at 9:45 P.M. "during one of the worst northeast gales and blinding snowstorms known in Digby's history." To compound the problem, a storm-bound Dominion Atlantic Railway train temporarily blocked firemen from crossing Sydney Street to fight the

rapidly-spreading inferno. An account in the February 17, 1899 *Digby Courier* reported the following details:

"Many of our leading citizens were enjoying themselves at the residence of Mayor Shreve, celebrating the tenth anniversary of his marriage when the alarm sounded. This broke up a very pleasant evening and the ladies and gentlemen were soon hurrying in all directions to reach home and look after their property, some of which was already surrounded by fire...."

"THE FIRE BURNED THROUGH THE NIGHT"

"The flames spread both ways on both sides of the street...and it was thought by many that we would lose the entire business portion of the town including some fine residences on Queen Street. The cold was intense and many of the citizens as well as the firemen were covered with ice. The fire continued to spread and dry goods, boots and shoes, house-hold furniture, show cases, etc. were being carried out of the adjoining buildings and piled in the streets, the increasing snowdrifts covering a large portion of the already damaged goods... The vacant lots on the east

side of the street greatly assisted the firemen whose attention could now be almost entirely given to the west side. Three-thirty Tuesday morning the fire was under control, and confined to the burning foundations. About this time the wind blew even harder and large snow-drifts filled the streets. The crowd began to disperse and seek shelter...."

The morning after

"At daylight, Water St. presented a sad sight, one not to be forgotten. The foundations were still slowly burning and the street was filled with furniture, dry goods, etc., half covered with snow drifts.... It is rumoured that some of the people who attended the fire are at present quite well supplied with dry goods, boots, shoes and groceries." Lost in the fire were G.I. Letteney & Brothers store; the Saunders building housing Guptil & Young, general merchants; Louie Komiesky's dry goods; the Wilson Block with S.M. Wilson's fruit & confectionary store and R.G. Monroe's law office; G.F. Stone's London House; Frank Jones's law office; Captain James Dillion's grocery store and residence; Mrs. McMullin's general provision store; Miss Georgie Beaman's bakery; Otis Warne's 'Bijou' confectionery store; Miss Janie Wright's millinery; the E.B. Nicholl's building with the law offices of Jones & Nicholls and H.L. Dennison, the sheriff's office, and Edmund Jenner's Drug Store; the George Bishop building with James H. McNeil tailors and George Trohon's barbershop; the Turnbull Block housing the post office and E. Turnbull's grocery; Mrs. B. Morse's stationery & fancy store (owned by T.S. Patillo & Company, Truro); Captain Fred Robinson's Restaurant; C.H. Young's Fruit & Confectionery; C.H. Lindstrom's jewelry store (upstairs was Dr. Morgan's dentist office); John Russell's harness shop and that of Edward Young, shoemaker; Waverly House; the Shreve Block with I.C. Shreve's law office, the town clerk's office, and H.B. Short's Boot & Shoe Store; Mrs. Louis Bacon's store and residence; Keen & Hutchinson's Carriage Factory and Undertaking Shop; and George Stailing & Sons Stables. In the final tally, 44 properties were destroyed or damaged, with 24 having no insurance coverage whatsoever. Total loss was estimated at $89,500 (insurance covered $33,100) with G.I. Letteney's store, the source of the fire, being the most heavily insured at $8,000.

Digby rebuilds

"Much credit must be given to our firemen and citizens, who labored so faithfully to save the town, and considering disadvantages under which they worked…it seemed almost a miracle that the fire did not cross Sydney Street and sweep the entire town." Within three days of the fire, the Digby Courier announced that it was 'business as usual' for the town. Many of the burned-out merchants and public officials had rented or were sharing retail and office space elsewhere while the formidable task of cleaning-up and rebuilding Digby's north end got underway. "To Mr. G.F. Stone belongs the honour of erecting the first building in the burnt district. It is a temporary structure to be used only until a more permanent building is erected. There is no unmixed evil and even as the result of our loss will come better buildings and a greatly improved street." This Water Street portrayl, c. 1905, depicts the new Letteney and Turnbull buildings, their false fronts inscribed with the year of the 'Big Fire'. Oswald Wright purchased the Letteney premises in 1924, opening a dry goods store that sold men's, women's, and children's clothing. In 1946 his son Norman joined the firm; when his father died in 1952, Norman continued to manage the store until it closed in 1968, shortly after which the building was demolished.

Awaiting election results

Digby residents crowd Water Street in front of the *Courier* office to await results from the 1911 federal election. Free trade between Canada and the United States was the central issue and, as evidenced by this photo, interest in town was high. The ruling Liberal party under Sir Wilfred Laurier touted reciprocity while the Conservative's Sir Robert Borden, with the rallying cry of "No truck with the Yankees," pushed for tariff protections. The country was split, Central Canada's manufacturers backing the Conservatives and many in the Maritime fishing communities favouring the Liberals. In the end, Laurier was defeated and free trade was dead. Three-quarters of a century later, it would be the Conservative party, under Prime Minister Brian Mulroney, that would strike a contentious free-trade agreement in 1988 with the United States.

ADMIRAL DIGBY MUSEUM

An early 1900s Paul Yates photo of the Jane Dakin House on Montague Row. The Georgian-style home is believed to have been built prior to 1840 and was last lived in around 1966. It was purchased in 1968 by the Admiral Digby Library and Historical Society, first serving as the town's library, and then—from 1972 to the present—as the Admiral Digby Museum.

Two of the town's oldest homes still in existence are believed to be the Rutherford house at 19 Warwick Street, and the McBride house at 15 Water Street. Both date to 1784. It was in the front room of Henry Rutherford's home that he and George Nash opened Digby's first store. Another early home still standing is the Lightfoot House at 164 Queen Street; when built in 1810 its plaster walls were made from a concoction of clam shells.

GREEN HOUSE, QUEEN STREET

In 1896, David F. Young designed this house at 157 Queen St. for Herbert Green, manager of the Bank of Nova Scotia. It served as a bank manager's residence for many years until it was sold in 1970. Noted Digby merchant and builder Israel Letteney also designed a number of elegant houses in and around the town in the late 1800s. Two examples of his work are found adjacent to the Green House at 159 and 161 Queen Street. Letteney's plans incorporated a variety of features, such as widow walks, turrets, brackets, gingerbread trim, and shingled facades. Several fine examples of Victorian-style homes built by Digby's affluent citizenry during the "building boom" of 1890-1910 can still be seen along present-day Queen Street. Jesse Keen, James Irvine, and Matthias Kelly were listed as builders among the earliest Loyalist settlers, with Lawrence Hortwicke as architect and house carpenter.

RIGHT

HOLDSWORTH TAVERN

The Holdsworth Tavern, built in the 1780s at 1 Water Street, was one of the oldest buildings in Digby until it was torn down in 1983 because of its deteriorated condition. Holdsworth's was a popular eighteenth century watering hole for carrying on business transactions and exchanging news and views. It was also used by the local militia to fortify their resolve before marching off to defend the town on those occasions when roving privateers were sighted in the Bay of Fundy. Although Digby never faced the guns of an attacker from the days of its founding, the need for vigilence was ever present; a settler was once briefly taken hostage by American pirates at Privateer Cove in Little Joggin, to the south of town. One can imagine the laughter over a grog at Holdsworth's when the militia returned from the

following military engagement during the War of 1812: "At one time a rumour became current that the Americans were about raiding Sissibou (Weymouth). The Militia officers quickly summoned their Company for practice, and that night stationed a Guard at Shook's Point. Before morning the sentries heard a crackling in the bushes. Fearing the enemy were upon them, they fired a volley in direction of the noise. Imagine their surprise and chagrin when they discovered they had shot and killed Deacon Shook's cow! For this valiant service some of the Company received a pension for life."

'LOBSTER SMACK' ON QUEEN STREET

Five yoke of oxen tow a "Lobster Smack" down Queen Street c. 1876. The small vessel was built by Martin Oliver, who had a boat works next door to his house on the corner of Warwick Street and Montague Row. A "smack" was a small decked or half-decked boat of various rig built primarily for fishing and usually having a live well in its hold. The procession appears to have been somewhat of a gala event, as a number of women and children are featured on deck while others line the route to watch the smack's passing. Andrew Thebault was identified as the lead teamster; Digby Neck's Will Ross—dressed in white hat, suspenders, and holding a switch at the rear—was described on the photo's back as being a "rough character."

CARRIAGE RIDE ALONG KING STREET

Digby offered a variety of scenic vistas for the visiting tourist or the traditional after-church Sunday drive. An early 1900s brochure listed the following routes: "Few resorts are favored with such a variety of really good roads for automobile or carriage. The 'shore road' skirting the Gap to Point Prim, on the rocky shores of Fundy, is a six-mile panorama of suberb scenery. The 'light-house road' to the bay is another fine drive. The Acacia Valley road leads through a region of rural beauty. The drive to Bear River, following the south shore of the Basin and the banks of the 'Rhine of Nova Scotia' is one of diversified and picturesque scenes. Other interesting points are at St. Mary's Bay, the 'French Shore' and Digby Neck."

STORM-TOSSED SCHOONER

In this eerie c. 1922 photo, the 341-ton tern schooner *Gertrude Parsons*—built in 1919 at Cheverie, N.S.—was captured after having been driven ashore along Water Street during a snowstorm. The Red Raven building is barely visible through the squalls in the distance. The *Digby Courier* carried a less-than-sympathetic article of its demise on May 8, 1931. "The old building known as the Red Raven ended its chequered career at an early hour Wednesday morning when kindly flames removed what had become an eye sore and a bore of construction. Probably no business building in town has housed a greater variety of enterprises or has had a greater number of tenants than the Red Raven. It has been an ice cream parlor several times, a tea room on many occasions, a meat market, grocery store, laundry, printing and newspaper office and what have you? But it seemed to be...a "hoodooed" building and we have never heard of a single business conducted in that building where the proprietor did not come out poorer than when he went in."

The town had acquired the Red Raven a few days before it burned, and the building was slated for demolition or moving to make way for rebuilding the breastworks after the March storm of 1931. The *Courier* concluded its piece by writing, "Some kind person saved the town the expense. It made a spectacular blaze and conditions were ideal for it."

South End Digby c. 1912

The wooden-fenced pastoral settings portrayed here have long since been lost in the pages of time and town development. Digby photographer Paul Yates took the panorama of south-end Digby from Lour Lodge, at the intersection of St. Mary's Street and First Avenue, using a telephoto lens. Records indicate that a racetrack was built on St. Mary's Street in 1787 near the Town Bridge. "Much enjoyment was derived by those engaged," writes Isaiah Wilson, "while immense capital exchanged hands in consequence. This Park however ended sadly. In a race, the driver of a horse owned by one of the contestants fell over the steed's head as the animal stumbled in his course and was instantly killed. The Park was thereafter

abandoned." When a quarter mile track opened in the early 1900s, interest in horse racing was revived. Blacksmith Henry Trask remembered how "every owner wanted the shoes made as light as possible. I once made a set for a racer owned by the late Dr. Frank Rice of Sandy Cove. They were made out of wagon tire steel and were so thin I had to braze on the caulks. The four shoes weighed less than a pound." Henry Trask began his trade at Digby in 1907 and was still active in 1959. Trask claimed that he and fellow blacksmith Fred Thebault once shoed an average of 18 cattle a day, the most being 23 in a single day.

SUMMER STROLL ALONG WATER STREET

No danger of speeding traffic here, as a woman enjoys a leisurely walk south along a shady section of Water Street. The house at right is said to have been owned at one time by Clarence Jameson, a prominent Digby citizen at the turn of the century. Born in 1872 at Bedeque, P.E.I., Clarence Jameson opened a law practice at Digby in 1893 and served as the town's Clerk and Treasurer from 1893-1908. In 1908, Jameson carried the federal seat for the Conservatives, winning re-election to

the House of Commons in 1911. He died on September 20, 1928. An earlier resident here was Brigadier-General Timothy Ruggles, who moved to Digby after the American War of Independence. Legend says that he initially supported the revolutionary forces, but he switched allegiances—which eventually cost him not only the first presidency of the United States, but also the life of his favourite daughter, who was hanged (with others) in retaliation. A number of buildings have occupied this site, including the present post office. Note the people seated on park benches to left in photo. This landscape would forever change with the March Storm of 1931.

MARCH STORM OF 1931

Headlines from the *Digby Courier*, Friday, March 6, 1931 told the devastating story portrayed here: "Tremendous Damage to Digby by Worst Storm in Years." "Wharves, Breastworks and Buildings Demolished, Great Damage to Embankments." "Water Street is Rendered Almost Impassable."

During a flood tide in the first week of March, Digby was battered for three hours by high seas and gale-force winds. Some buildings, built on pilings over the water, survived the onslaught but still suffered extensive damage from waves and storm-tossed debris, which lifted and buckled floors on lower levels. The public pavilion near the bandstand was undermined, toppling into the harbour, and the adjacent boat slip was washed away. Old wharves at the Racquette were destroyed and the Racquette Bridge—which had just been replaced after the August Gales of 1927—was again in need of extensive repairs. As a precautionary measure, Dominion Atlantic Railway freight cars had been removed from the Government Wharf before the height of the storm. This proved a wise decision as logs and wreckage were hurled onto the pier and into the streets. The ferry *Princess Helene* made the Bay of Fundy crossing safely from Saint John into the Annapolis Basin, but was unable to dock at Digby and was forced to seek shelter in the lee of North Mountain, near the Granville shore.

REPAIRING WATER STREET

After the storm, people immediately began to rebuild the sea walls and breastworks along Water Street; this work continued for several weeks. The town borrowed $51,000 to help defray the costs, a substantial amount in the Dirty Thirties. Survey lines were marked off, increasing the distance fifteen feet further out than the previous abuttments, and the March 27 issue of the *Digby Courier* reported that "The proposed new work will show a vast improvement in the appearance of the front street."

The house on the extreme right of the photograph was built c. 1784 at 15 Water Street with materials brought from Boston at the time of settlement. Long time residence of John Frederick McBride, and still owned today by McBride descendents, the Digby landmark has served many purposes, from an early stage coach stop to a social gathering spot, with ballroom dancing and boxing matches taking place on the second floor. During World War II the McBride House, then owned by Charles McBride, a member of the Digby Civic Band, hosted such musical legends as Louis Armstrong, Jimmy Dorsey, and Cab Colloway, who entertained forces personnel at nearby H.M.C.S. Cornwallis.

Every community had at least one well-known 'man about town' who endeared himself to the residents and visitors alike. Hardy Bent was Digby's claim to fame, so much so that he appeared on a 1921 postcard with the following descriptive poem, composed by T.F. Anderson of Boston. Bent, who lived on Mount Street, was more commonly known as Hardy 'Peg' in reference to an infirmity that required he walk with crutches. From the early 1870s until the 1930s, his shoeshine stand near the *Digby Courier* and Royal Hotel was a common sight on Water Street.

Ode to Hardy Bent

Since '71, in fashion neat
He's shined the shoes of Digby's feet.
He's scanned a hundred thousand faces
And sold a million miles of laces;
You'll find him "shining" hard and late
Close by the local Fourth Estate.
The shoes he's brushed, if packed in cars,
Would reach from here clear up to Mars.

He shines for Tories, Grits, and tramps,
And knows a lot concerning "vamps";
Likewise the tongues of (shoes and women)
And "Louis" heels and footwear trimmin'.
He'll polish up your auto "shoe"
As slick as one of kangaroo.
Of styles and "lasts" he knows the vogue,
And kens a brogan from a "brogue."

He's shined the shoes of Howes and Tuppers
And knows when we are "on our uppers."
He's filled with orthopedic knowledge,
And tho' he never went to college
He ranks high as an Oxford "grad"
And makes our summer tourists glad.
He's interested in their "rolls"
But bothers little with their soles.

We hope to meet him by-and-by,
Where living costs are not so high;
But Hardy will outshine us all,
For he'll receive St. Peter's call
To burnish with celestial fire
The sandals of the Heavenly Choir.
So let us quaff a cheering cup
To Hardy, whilst he shines 'em up!

William Bacon's produce wagons loaded with squash on Water Street, 1917, photographed by Paul Yates. From county historian Isaiah Wilson we learn that very early on "many farmers had become nearly independent from abundant crops and sale of stock, together with proceeds of the sea and forests....When organization to promote agriculture was proposed, Digby soon accepted that experiment."

The first efforts date to 1819, when the Digby Agricultural Society was organized. Its mandate included the entire Western District of Annapolis County, of which Digby was then still a part. This society continued for 20 years until an 1840 meeting in Acacia Valley formed the Hillsburgh Agricultural Society. It was hoped this new organization would better serve Digby's farmers by "introducing stock, seeds, implements of husbandry, books and papers on farming and kindred topics." The Digby Central Agricultural Society was active by 1856, comprised at times of more than one hundred members, and continued until the early 1900s, at which time it was the "senior institution of its nature in the County." This society has been credited with holding the first Exhibitions within the county, usually at the junction of Faulkner Road and the old Post Highway from Digby to Annapolis, or in Marshalltown near Hill Grove Road and Cross Street. Similar agricultural societies were established between 1866-1879 at Clare, Weymouth, St. Mary's Bay, and again at Hillsburgh, leading to "immense progress in stock, fruit and other valuable branches (with) large profits being realized from those improvements, now deemed indispensable."

First automobiles

A Stanley Steamer driven by Paul Yates (L) and Charles Lindstrom in front of
Yates's photography studio on Water Street, 1911. George Wilson was reportedly
the first to own a motor vehicle in Digby, a 1906 Ford. Sheriff Guy Dunn
purchased the third automobile, a chain drive 1908 Reo. In 1909 his wife became
one of the first women drivers in the county. Digby residents paid Guy 50 cents
for the privilege of a five-mile drive around town in the newfangled contraption.
A driver's licence was not required in the early years and the first licence plates were
made by the owner; the government issued a number, which was then inscribed
onto a home-made plate and attached to the vehicle. As late as 1921 Nova Scotia
had not yet followed other provinces, and continued the British custom of driving
on the left side of the road. Town streets were first prepared for paving in the
spring of 1935; by July of that year the *Digby Courier* reported that paving was
"progressing satisfactorily."

Chapter 2

Business & Industry

SOUTH END GROCERY c. 1880

"South End Grocery Store; W.F. Turnbull. A Choice Assortment of Groceries Always on Hand. By a system of small profits our rapidly increasing business enables us to dispose of Best Family Groceries at astonishingly low figures. Call, price and inspect the Groceries at the South End before purchasing elsewhere." (*Digby Courier*, 1891)

Captain William Forsythe Turnbull opened his South End Grocery in the 1850s. Henry G. Turnbull, in white coat and cap, took over the business which he had been managing for a number of years when his father died in 1892. He put up a new building in 1896 on the corner of Warwick and Queen Streets, which was reported at the time to be "a modern store, with modern appointments...and makes an appearance very creditable to the town and proprietor."

DIGBY SHIPYARDS

A rare photo of a Digby shipyard depicts a large vessel on the stocks in the far distance, across from the Baptist church on Water Street. "The unrivalled materials found in Digby's forests," writes historian Isaiah Wilson, "coupled with its proximity to St. John, New Brunswick, the similarity in class and numerous relationships between residents of those centres, led to constant commercial and social intercourse. Many fine craft of huge dimensions were built in Digby for St. John merchantmen. Even some found their way to distant climes." Among the first Loyalist settlers were master shipbuilders Ebenezer and Samuel Street, master shipbuilder Leveret Bishop, ship carpenters Charles Richards and David Standish, and sail makers Daniel and James Leonard. Digby was reported to have three shipyards in 1845, these being at Joggin, the Racquette, and near Dakin's blacksmith shop. The latter may have been owned by James Jones, whose master builder was Daniel Dakin. In Frederick William Wallace's book *Wooden Ships and Iron Men*, Digby shipbuilders listed for the 1850-60s were William Hicks, Jeremiah Everitt, Edward J. Budd, Ira Raymond, and G.H. Dakin. In 1854, Edward J. Budd built the 1166-ton *John Owens* for Saint John interests, the second largest vessel constructed that year in Nova Scotia. R. M. Raymond & Sons owned a shipyard in later years and in 1876 constructed the 1226-ton *Marion* for A.C. Robbins. The 1,498-ton *Beaconsfield* was built in 1877 for John Stewart of Saint John, N.B. There is no mention of shipbuilding at Digby after the 1870s; however, even though the era of large square riggers in Nova Scotia had passed by the mid-1890s a number of Digby County shipyards continued turning out small tonnage schooners and barquentines into the early 1900s.

TRADE AND COMMERCE

This 1910 photo taken at the Government Wharf features a mosaic of masts, rigging and cross-trees. In the foreground are the three-masted schooners *Flora Condon* of Boston (left) and the *Catherine*, 196 tons, built in 1903 at Meteghan River, Digby County. By the early 1800s, Digby had "an extensive trade in timber, lumber and fish, coupled with sugar, molasses and spirituous liquors was followed with the West Indies. Hard and soft cordwood were manufactured throughout the County except islands and exported to Boston and Massachusetts and other parts in New England States."

One of the earliest firms on record in Digby "for prosecuting an extensive business in shipping and commerce" was Bonnell & Budd, established in January 1794 by Isaac Bonnell and Elisha Budd. In partnership with Ambrose Haight and John Stewart, they purchased a quarter interest in the schooner *Ferebee and Phoebe* for the West Indian trade. Convinced that the schooner was too small for their interests, the firm "constructed at great cost" a copper-fastened vessel, the *Queen Charlotte*. Loaded with timber, fish and lumber, she sailed in the autumn of 1805 for Barbados under the command of Captain Adam Walker. This venture ended in tragedy: "time passed; no tidings came. At length all was abandoned in despair. The noble merchantman with all on board had evidently become a prey to the unknown."

Re-decking "Long Wharf"

At the time of this 1910 Paul Yates photo, Long Wharf—including the spur wharf in background—was known as Steamboat Pier or, more commonly, the Government Wharf. Being the terminus for Digby's trade and commerce and the Saint John ferry, these wharves would have been in need of constant maintenance and repair (as seen here). The first government-funded wharf built on this site was contracted out to J.L. Mayes from Saint John, N.B. c. 1878. Prior to this, vessels offloaded at low tide into row boats, which conveyed passengers and freight to a long slipway extending beyond the low water mark. Andrew's Wharf (near the bandstand) was used at times of high tide and, being ill-equipped for such rigorous demands, was said to have made disembarkation something of an adventure. In 1918, Digby is reported to have had 16 wharves along its waterfront.

COAL SHEDS

A schooner lies alongside the coal wharf at low tide, c. 1920. In the distance is the Government Wharf with its freight and terminal buildings. The two coal sheds pictured here were built c. 1880, with braced walls that sloped in at the top for added strength. Many early stoves and fireplaces burned coal. In the 1890s, H.B. Allen ran advertisements in the Digby Courier for hard and soft coal from Sydney, Springhill, and Joggins. From his office in the Shreve building on Water Street, W.E. (Will) Van Blarcom operated a coal supply business on this wharf in the early 1900s. The vessel is unidentified but could be the *Westway*, built at Weymouth, Digby County, in 1918. This three-master served as a coal freighter until wrecked on Gull Rock in St. Mary's Bay on November 8, 1925. Partway up the foreward mast, in the photo, is a boom with pulley, used to hoist buckets of coal from the ship's hold to a loading hole visible in the building's roof. The coal sheds were later renovated and used from 1936-1979 by Snow Brothers fish business. One of the buildings is still standing today as part of Tidal Boatworks. An interesting feature of this photo are the expansive mud flats, which illustrate the dramatic rise and fall of Fundy's twice-daily tides; at Digby, these tides can vary as much as 30 feet in six-and-a-half hours.

DIGBY WATERFRONT

Isaiah Wilson writes that in the late 1800s "shipbuilding was rendered unprofitable...by the rapid transit powers of steamers which were constructed in St. John, N.B. and other principal marts....Digby almost overwhelmingly afflicted soon found relief through greater attention to the deep sea fisheries, and this very profitable industry developed rapidly. The firms of Syda & Cousins, D.&O. Sproul, John W. Snow, with smaller concerns, netted immense profits and became quite independent." An 1897 issue of the *Digby Courier* reiterates the importance of fishing to Digby's economy: "There are many in different parts of Digby County who are entirely dependent upon the resources of the sea and whose life avocation has been to sail the deep and throw the line. We are a maritime county and our fishing ranks third largest in the province.... The fishing business managed from Digby town totals nearly $100,000 per year...and some two hundred men are employed."

In this c.1908 photo, several schooners are berthed dockside at what is thought to be the Syda-Cousins fish processing plant and wharves. H.P. Robertson of Saint John, N.B. purchased the property and wholesale fish business in 1910, following the death of John H. Syda and the retirement of Captain James W. Cousins. Visible to the left are the Cannon Banks, with its white rows of fish curing on drying racks. To the right is a Dominion Atlantic Railway locomotive on the Government Wharf. This may have been a "shunter," used to move passenger and freight cars back and forth between the train station and ferry terminal. Little remains today as testament to this busy waterfront scene except some crumbling cribworks of logs and stone, visible at low tide. In its place are the buildings of O'Neil Fisheries, Casey Fisheries, a marina, and Fishermen's Wharf.

In-Shore fishery

The Digby fishery was described in the August 1914 issue of the *Canadian Fisherman*: "The fish are caught by a growing fleet of, at present, ten sailing vessels averaging about ninety tons each, which fish offshore; several smaller sailing vessels of about twenty-five tons, fitted with marine engines, which are used in gathering the fares of the fishermen of out-lying places along the shores; and a fleet of small, open, motor boats of the finest class built. The boats and smaller vessels fish along the shores of the Bay of Fundy, often but a short distance from Digby Gap and frequently right in the [Annapolis] Basin."

The "seine" type of net that's featured here was hung vertically in the water, with floats along its top edge and weights at the bottom. It was generally set in 20-30 feet of water to catch herring or mackerel. Digby herring were "celebrated wherever known" and when smoked were marketed as 'Digby Chickens,' a term which legend says originated with the founding Loyalists who, lacking feathered delicacies, dined regularly on herring. Reports indicate that "immense quantities" of Digby Chickens were exported in the 1880s, but by the early 1900s smoked herring production had "dwindled down to practically nil"—due in large measure to the rapid growth of the finnan haddie business.

S.S. "Prince Rupert," entering the Gap, Digby, N.S.

FISHING WEIR AT DIGBY GUT

A "weir" is an intricate fishing enclosure made from poles, brush, and twine; the herring swim into this enclosure, become entrapped, and are then netted by fishermen in small boats or scooped up at low tide. Weirs have been traced back thousands of years, and were a common sight along the Annapolis Basin well into the mid-1900s. Sources tell us that "weirs were built at a very early period, every available location speedily occupied. Many even neglected their farms to follow this occupation exclusively." The weir fishery was considered so important that on November 3, 1784, Digby residents met to adopt a number of protective regulations. Most dealt with restricting the use of set and sweep nets within certain distances of weirs. One interesting clause stipulated "that any weir within the Basin of Annapolis, in which three barrels of dead or odious fish be found remaining twenty-four hours, the owner thereof shall pay the sum of Five Pounds, one-half of which shall go to the informer, and the residue to Overseers of the Poor in the Parish, in which the particular weir shall be situated."

FINNAN HADDIE

In this photo, the man wearing a bowler hat and salting finnan haddie was Andrew Tebo, a familiar sight on the Digby docks, whose years of hard work reportedly allowed him to light a pipe from matches struck on the palms of his calloused hands. The August 1914 issue of the *Canadian Fisherman* touted Digby as "the prime finnan haddie manufacturing town in the Maritime Provinces." Finnan haddie are smoked haddock. The term comes from Findhorn haddock, Findhorn being the Scottish fishing port where the process originated. John Austin is credited with introducing smoked finnan haddie to Canada; Digby is said to have been the first town to market them. Austin was a Scottish barber who emigrated with his family to Smith's Cove, Digby County in 1856 and began his finnan haddie business two years later. He was followed into the fish trade by his son Robert Austin, a sea captain, who in 1884 expanded into canned finnan haddie. From a company wharf in Smith's Cove, his Thistle Brand trademark was shipped as far away as the West Indies. The Austins moved their business in 1887 to Little River on Digby Neck, where fish were reported to be more abundant.

MARITIME FISH CORPORATION, 1910

Alfred H. Brittain began his career in the retail fish trade in 1904, marketing boneless and shredded codfish. Soon realizing this venture was too narrow in scope, he and a number of prominent businessmen in Montreal and the Maritime Provinces "expanded into a proposition to tackle the whole field of the fish trade—fresh, smoked, boneless, salted and dried—and organized the Maritime Fish Corporation in 1910." In need of East Coast ports from which to operate, the Montreal-based company bought out the two Digby fishing firms of Short & Ellis and Captain Howard Anderson, as well as Canso's A.N. Whitman & Sons. Using existing wharves and fish plants, and constructing a number of new buildings, Maritime Fish Corporation opened their Digby operation in 1910 at the Racquette. Records for the month of April 1914 alone show the Maritime Fish Corporation processing 233,351 lb of haddock; 398,009 lb of cod; 8,487 lb of cusk; 2,009 lb of halibut; and 800 lb of hake. For 30 years Maritime Fish competed with Halifax's National Fish Company as the premier producers and distributers of fish products in Nova Scotia. In 1929 the two combatants were merged into Maritime National Fish, run out of Halifax. Following a re-structuring and change of ownership in 1937, Maritime National Fish became part of National Sea Products in 1945, which continued to operate the Digby plant until the plant was sold, in 1986, to Kenny Fisheries from Digby Neck.

SALT & PICKLING DEPT. AT MARITIME FISH CORPORATION

Maritime Fish Corporation's Digby branch was an impressive operation. The *Digby Courier* of December 30, 1910 reported that "their buildings have been put up so rapidly along with the wharf extensions and other improvements...that many of our regular residents have but a slight idea of the large sums of money which have been spent in the Racquette since last August and the rush of business which is being carried on daily at the north end." The article describes in great detail the "splendidly furnished" company offices and general store stocked with groceries, fishing supplies, and marine hardware. Listed were the many new and renovated buildings which housed dressing rooms, salt and pickling departments, and a fresh fish warehouse. There were two smokehouses and large packing rooms for finnan haddie, and a three-storey building used exclusively for the dry fish trade. Added to this were two hot air drying rooms "where fish can be cured in any kind of weather," a vegetable cellar for provisioning vessels, and the convenience of electricity throughout the entire plant. Maritime Fish Corporation's Digby branch officers were listed as manager Harry Short (prior owner of Short & Ellis); Miss May Whynacht, secretary; Captain Howard Anderson, superintendent; James Ellis, foreman; Joseph F. Milberry, manager of the company's store; Frank Anderson, shipping clerk. Special note was made of the fact that "between 45 and 50 men are kept continually on the pay roll, each of whom was presented with a turkey by their employers Christmas Eve."

THE RACQUETTE

The Racquette, no doubt named for its circular shape, is a protected cove just to the north of town, and is the site of some of Digby's earliest wharves and shipbuilding activity. Prior to Loyalist settlement in 1783, Christopher Prince from Boston built a trading post at the Racquette c. 1766 and "prosecuted an extensive trade, largely with the Indians, for some years." To the left in this panorama (viewed from the Pines Hotel) are the buildings and wharves of Maritime Fish Corporation's plant. Next door, on the right, was D. & O. Sproul's wholesale fish business, which in the late 1890s annually shipped three thousand barrels of dry fish to Havana,

nine hundred cases of live lobsters to Boston and eight thousand cases of finnan haddies as far west as Winnipeg. D. & O. Sproul also held half ownership in the Digby Canning Company, which processed twenty thousand cans of lobster per year. Much of the firm's success was attributed to its telegraph-order business and the expediency by which their product reached markets.

The tents at the foreground in bottom right are in the area where native Mi'kmaq routinely camped along the Racquette during summer months to fish and clam, and to make baskets, trinkets, and woodenware for the tourist market.

DRYING FISH ON THE CANNON BANKS

Digby had four principal areas for drying fish. One of the largest was at the Cannon Banks, on land once reserved for a planned 250-room hotel which never materialized and, in 1904, reverted to fish lots. Drying racks—or "flakes"—were also at the Maritime Fish Corporation, which was in the vicinity of the present Nova Scotia Liquor Commission; other flakes were at the north end of King and Queen Streets; still others were at various wharves along the Racquette. Cod, hake, and pollock were the most common species dried. During the drying process, which generally required three weeks, fish would be taken from the flakes and stacked into large press piles (featured here at bottom right) to squeeze out what moisture remained before being laid out again to finish curing.

Digby's fish wholesalers reported 1903 to have been a particularly good year, listing the following exports: Short & Ellis—500,000 lb of haddock and 150,000 lb of mixed fish; Captain Joseph Snow—200,000 lb of "Digby Chickens" (smoked herring) and 500,000 lb of mixed fish; Syda & Cousins—650,000 lb mixed fish; D. & O. Sproul—700,000 lb mixed fish; Anderson & Letteney—605,000 lb of hake and haddock, 102,000 lb of cod.

FISHING SCHOONER *DOROTHY G. SNOW*, C. 1911

One of Digby's best known fishing schooners was the *Dorothy G. Snow*, built in 1911 at Joseph McGill's Shelburne shipyard. A typical design for that era, the 98-ton vessel was owned by Captain Joseph E. Snow, a retired Digby fishing skipper who operated one of the town's largest fresh and smoked fish companies. Named in honour of his daughter Dorothy Greeley Snow, the ship's first captain was Joseph's brother, William Snow. The schooner had a remarkable 50-year career, still sailing in 1960 out of St. Vincent, Cape Verde Island in Portuguese West Africa. Under new ownership and re-named the *Maria Sonia*, she survived not only a two-week battering in an Atlantic gale, but, at 49 years of age, went on to win a seven hundred mile race against two other schooners, beating her nearest rival by eighteen hours.

Unlike Lunenburg's celebrated fishing fleet of 140 salt bankers from Nova Scotia's south shore, the modest number of vessels sailing from Digby were 'fresh fishermen' that carried large quantities of ice instead of salt to preserve their catch. Whereas Lunenburg struggled to hold onto a century's old salt-fishing tradition into the early 1900s, Digby adapted to the changing market demands for fresh fish: "the larger vessels do their summer fishing around the mouth of the Bay of Fundy on the grounds known as the German Banks or the Seal Island grounds, where they catch principally hake, cusk, cod and haddock. About the first of February, they change their grounds and follow the fish further south to Brown's, LaHave and Western Banks, where the catch is principally haddock; the great bulk of the haddock caught during the winter months comes from Brown's Bank which is situated about fifty miles south of Cape Sable, N.S." Some Digby captains also ventured into the Gulf of St. Lawrence to fish halibut, which brought the highest prices. To ensure a product suitable for the fresh or frozen market on trips that could possibly last three weeks, vessels often unloaded catches at the Maritime Fish Corporation's Canso facilities.

CAPTAIN ANSEL SNOW AT THE WHEEL OF THE *DOROTHY G. SNOW*

Captain Ansel Snow, brother of Joseph and William Snow, established a record catch for Digby fishing schooners in November 1912, when his vessel the *Dorothy G. Snow* returned to port with a one-day catch of sixty thousand pounds of fish. He achieved this mark despite being four crewmen and two dories short of a full complement.

Frederick William Wallace, who sailed with Ansel Snow while gathering material for his book *Roving Fisherman* described the skipper as having "the reputation of being a 'driver' and men who shipped with Ansel had to forget about resting or sleeping if it was fishing weather. There were many who wouldn't sail with him. He worked his gangs hard. But if his men toiled overtime, so did he. Out of Digby, Yarmouth, and Gloucester, Massachusetts, he had skippered vessels in all kinds of fishing ever since he was a young man. He was what they called 'a hard fisherman'."

EFFIE M. MORRISSEY

Digby's "little fleet of schooners" included the *Albert J. Lutz, Dorothy M. Smart, Loran B. Snow, Wilfred L. Snow, Alcyone, Cora May, Myrtle L, Eddie J., Defender,* and the *Robert & Arthur.* There were also several American-built schooners that were Digby-owned and Digby-crewed, but were registered in the United States: *Quickstep, Harvester, Samuel R. Crane, Oliver Killam, Effie M. Morrissey, Grace Darling.* These US-registered vessels were permitted by law to land their fish in the lucrative U.S. market without paying duty, a luxury not then afforded Canadian registered vessels. In February 1901, the *Quickstep*, commanded by Captain Arthur Casey from nearby Victoria Beach, reportedly landed the first catch of haddock ever taken by a Digby vessel on the Brown's Bank.

Another famous vessel with Digby connections was the 120-foot schooner *Effie M. Morrissey*, built in 1894 in Essex, Massachusetts for Captain William E. Morrissey of Gloucester. For 30 years she fished the Grand Banks, sailing for different owners and captains. In March 1905, the *Effie M. Morrissey* was bought by Ansel Snow, who fished the schooner out of Digby until 1909. In 1912 Captain Harry Ross bought shares in the "Effie" and, with a Digby crew, made frequent trips into Portland and Boston with fresh fish. She was sold to American interests in 1924, refitted, then sent north on a series of Arctic explorations. She was sold again in 1948 to Hendrique Mendes of the Cape Verde Islands, who renamed her the *Ernestina.* For nearly three decades she served as an Atlantic packet, ferrying passengers and freight between Africa and America. After extensive restoration in 1982, the 88-year old vessel "was given by the people of Cape Verde to the people of the United States for educational, cultural and community development purposes," a role she currently continues to fulfill.

DORY CREW OF THE *DOROTHY M. SMART*

Dorymen Jim Tidd (left) and Judson Handspiker enjoy a smoke break amid trawl tubs in this 1911 Frederick William Wallace photo. Fishermen who manned Digby vessels hailed from all parts of the county, as well as from communities like Victoria Beach, Port Wade, Parker's Cove, Hillsburn, Young's Cove and Litchfield on the Annapolis County side of the Basin. Some came from neighbouring Yarmouth County, while others came from as far away as Newfoundland. Frederick William Wallace wrote of a custom introduced to Digby vessels by Newfoundland fishermen: "When lying-to in a gale and seeing a big sea roll up towards the vessel, they [Newfoundlanders] were in the habit of making a Sign of the Cross in front of the advancing comber and murmuring: "May the Cross of Christ come between you and us!" This ritual of averting the menace of a threatening wave was known as 'Crossing the Seas'."

It was customary for Digby fishing crews to work on "even shares," though some captains prefered a "by-the-count" method—meaning each man was paid according to the number of fish he caught. Fishing in the early 1900s was even then a speculative business and it could be either feast or famine for wages despite the fact an average trip of 5 to 15 days generally resulted in a catch of 60,000 — 120,000 pounds of fish. In 1912, a ten-day trip to Brown's Bank netted each man $77; on another trip of 13 days, a catch of mostly haddock cleared a crewman $55; both sums were considered "a good return for those days." On the downside, one 1915 Digby crew, after a two-week trip of poor weather and scarce fish, each pocketed just $5, leaving only enough for "bare smoking money, and some didn't have that."

DIGBY FROM THE GOVERNMENT WHARF

Looking west from Government Wharf, the prominent rooftop "Jaeger" sign was an advertising ploy to entice passengers arriving via the Saint John-Digby ferry to shop at Wright's Clothing Store on Water Street, which carried an extensive Jaeger line of fine British woollens. The open expanse on the hill in the distance was a nine-hole golf course operated by the Digby Golf Club from 1915-1939.

The long pier in foreground is Anderson's Wharf, known possibly for the early 1900s fishing firm of Anderson & Letteney. Coasting vessels and packets docked at Anderson's and later c. 1940s the British American Oil Company supplied vessels with gas, oil, and water from pumps at the end of the wharf. The small building was used at one time for a clamming business by Soffron Brothers from Ipswitch, Massachusetts. Digby clams processed here were said to have been packed into tins and exported south of the border, stamped as a U.S. product. Shellfish played an important role in Digby's sea-based economy, with thousands of barrels of lobsters and "large quantities" of winkles and mussels shipped in season. The August 1914 issue of the *Canadian Fisherman* noted that "the clam industry in Digby should not be overlooked" citing average annual exports of 10,000 barrels. "These clams are the soft shell variety, of excellent quality and find a ready market in the United States. The Canadian markets do not seem to appreciate them except in a shocked state, and then the quantity used is not great. In the rush seasons upwards of one hundred men are constantly employed, and two or three hundred barrels are shipped daily."

DIGBY SCALLOPS

The Pines Hotel backdrops this c. 1930 photo of an early scallop boat and three-masted schooner moored dockside at the Racquette. Digby scallops, long famed as a "gourmet's delight," are relatively recent in the historical context of the town's

fishery. For many years, local fishermen were aware of scallops in the Annapolis Basin and Bay of Fundy as the shellfish frequently became entangled in nets. However, it was not until about 1906 that Digby fisherman Captain Roland Wormell is credited with pioneering the first efforts to harvest scallops commercially. With a borrowed hand-rake drag from a blacksmith in Chester (where inshore fishermen had dragged scallops for some years previous) Captain Wormell and an associate, W.W. Hayden, landed 13 scallops on their first attempt. Fishing from a 35-foot decked-over sloop powered by a four-cylinder engine, their second trip produced 26 scallops. Still, until the 1920s, interest in fishing scallops commercially for export was slow to develop. John W. Hayden joined the enterprising fishermen and, with two drags built by Digby blacksmith A.J. Trohon (and patented in 1926 by Captain Wormell as the Digby Scallop Rake), the trio harvested a whopping six hundred scallops—which then posed a marketing problem. With local fish wholesalers hesitant to handle an unknown product, Captain James Ellis urged the fishermen, in 1922, to ship 55 pounds in wooden kegs to Gloucester on a trial basis. With a return of $2.50 a U.S. gallon (equal to nine pounds of scallops), interest rapidly grew, leading to a Digby scallop fleet that once numbered more than a hundred vessels. In the 1950s scallop fishermen received 40-cents a pound at dockside, and by 1970 $500,000 in scallops were landed by Digby fishermen, making it the town's principal industry. A curious scallop tale from the early days: when Captain Wormell and his mates first made scallop chowder from the rims, the men became ill, not realizing that the muscled hinge joining the two shell halves was the only edible part. When the chowder was fed to cats, the animals developed paralysis.

In 1845, Digby's 12 stores served a population of eight hundred. Unlike Otis Warne's 1900s confectionary pictured here, showcases were then non-existent, as were plate glass windows, and shopkeepers kept money at home in a strong box

because there were no banks in town. Some merchants identified for the 1840s were Edwin Marshall, George Bragg, James Crowley, James Randolph, Captain Payson, and the partnerships of Viets & Longley and Churchill & Taylor.

By the mid-1800s, the number of shopkeepers had grown to include James H. Fitzrandolph, William Burnham, Edward J. Budd, Edward M. Marshall, Edwin R. Oakes, John R. Mead, William F. Turnbull, Luke Quinn, Robert S. Fitzrandolph, George Henderson, Edwin Bent, Daniel L. Burnham, Charles Pinkney, R. M. Raymond & Sons, Thomas Master, James Keen, J.E. Young, Charles Master, George Brooks. Prominent names of the 1890s were Dakin Brothers, Edmund Burnham, G.I. Letteney & Bro., J.F. Saunders, Guptill & Young, J.L. Peters, Turnbull & Welsh, Smith & Allen, H.G. Turnbull, C.R.S. Mason, C.W. Muise, H.B. Short, and Robert E. Feltus.

DAKIN BROTHERS TINSMITHS, HARDWARE, KITCHEN FURNISHERS

A display of stoves line the front of Charles Dakin's counter at Dakin Brothers store on Water Sreet. In 1878, Charles and Henry Dakin paid $760 for the tinsmith business of Milton Anderson; they began to manufacture stoves and stove piping, and to repair kettles, pots, and pans. Charles was the more experienced of the two brothers, having learned the tinsmith trade while living for a time in Boston. Dakin Brothers was an aggressive firm, the brothers peddling their wares door to door from an ox cart. From the outset it was a money-making business, financial records for the first three days of operation showing revenues of $1.85 with expenditures of only $0.30; within sixteen months Dakin Brothers had a cash balance of $547. From these humble beginnings, the firm became one of Digby's most successful businesses—owing in large measure to the brothers' entrepreneural skills. In 1880 they added the highly touted Burnett and Johnson line of stoves to their inventory and, in 1883, branched into the plumbing business, making pumps. When Digby installed waterworks in the 1890s, Dakin Brothers was at the fore, hiring a Newfoundland plumber by the name of Shaw to lay water lines to homes attached to the new system. And in 1900, to meet consumer demand, the firm increased considerably its line of small hardware. Their advertising was just as skillful: from its inception in 1878, Dakin Brothers carried weekly advertisements in the *Digby Courier,* one of its more "novel advertising campaigns" being a weekly "Free Gift Day." A May 4, 1906 advertisement read: "We have selected for our Free Gift Day, April 14. Look up your receipts and if you have any showing that date come to our store on Tuesday, May 15 and get your money back." Dakin Brothers were also one of the first in Digby to sell radios, doing a large business in early models.

DAKIN BROTHERS OFFICE

An unidentified man jots notes as Charles Dakin relaxes in the office of Dakin
Brothers store. Without the luxury of computerized inventories and business
records, Dakin must have spent long hours keeping meticulous accounts in the
ledgers which line the back wall. Company books show a veritable who's who of
Digby, listing sea captains, vessel owners, doctors, judges, merchants, hotel keepers,
ministers, and Commissioners of both the Digby Gaol and the Western Counties
Railway. Business came from nearby Weymouth and Tiverton, and as far away as
Yarmouth, Halifax, and Saint John, N.B. On November 17, 1879 Captain John
Raymond purchased a Victor stove, iron kettle, boiler, fry pan, and bake tin from
Dakin Brothers for the sum total of $26.00.

The brother partnership came to an end in 1904 when Henry left the firm
and went into business for himself. Charles retained the Dakin Brothers name and
in 1907 took his son Fritz into the company; Fritz had already worked as a clerk
since 1899. When Charles passed away in 1924, Fritz Dakin carried on for many
years after, maintaining the family tradition of managing "one of Digby's most
progressive stores."

LETTENEY BROTHERS

Boardwalk sales at Letteney Brothers store on Water Street. G. Israel Letteney
established this business in 1871, later taking on his brother Jonathan as a partner.
By 1897, G.I. Letteney & Brother ranked "as one of the most thoroughly known
and best advertised business houses in three counties...(and) are in a position which
rivals the largest city establishment." Letteney Brothers had the biggest store in
Digby, its four floors featuring an array of general merchandise, fine dry goods,
house furnishings, and a tailoring department. G.I. Letteney also managed the
Letteney Manufacturing Company in nearby Brighton, which produced "Comet"
stove polish, blueing, lumber lead pencils, ink, muscilage, harness oil, and leather
cement. Comet stove polish had a reputation "over the entire Dominion," while
other products sold "far and near and have earned a name and a record for standard
merit." The Letteney firm was also heavily involved in shipping, and operated a
regular packet service between Digby and Saint John, N.B.

EBER TURNBULL'S GROCERY STORE

Patrons at Eber Turnbull's grocery store seek warmth from a central radiator amid signs advertising Blatchford's Calf Meal, Five Roses Flour, Minard's Linament, Moir's Chocolates, Ogilvie's Royal Household Flour and Reindeer Milk. In 1883, the Truro Condensed Milk & Canning Company became the first in Canada to manufacture condensed milk. Within a year the company was marketing two hundred thousand cans annually, under the Reindeer brand name—"Richest & Best Jersey Cream."

J. L. PETERS STORE

In 1874, J. Loran Peters (standing in the foreground next to the counter) moved from Westport to Digby and went to work for Robert S. Fitzrandolph, who had established a dry-goods store in 1852. Peters bought the business when Fitzrandolph died, opening a second shop, in the building next door, where he sold carpets. J.L. Peters was considered the "plate glass pioneer" of store windows in town, making his establishment "one of the attractions of Digby."

DIGBY BOOK STORE

The woman carrying newspapers in this photo is identified as possibily being Roxina Cousins, the proprietor of Digby Book Store. Note the window advertisement for the *New York Herald*. With the Compulsory Education Act of 1864 and subsequent improvements in education, "Literature became more generally read and appreciated," writes Isaiah Wilson. "The first Bookstore in the County was shortly opened at Digby by Miss Austin; the foreign newspapers increased their circulation rapidly; the Examiner and its successors were very generally patronized; and the rising generation with those coming after, received knowledge varied, useful and thorough, which their ancestors never obtained, because not within reach. Self-confidence was imparted and strengthened, which developed talents otherwise doomed to oblivion."

TONSORIAL PARLOR

Billy Cahoon's barbershop, later owned by Percy Keen. Note the ornate tin ceiling and the numbered shaving mugs. Barbershops were commonly referred to as "tonsorial parlors" in light of their reputation to solve world problems during the course of a single haircut. A moniker often used in reference to a barber was that of "tonsorial artist." George Trohon was an early Digby barber who lost his business in the fire of 1899, but he relocated to the upper floor of H.B. Short's shoe store on Water Street (later Arch Dillion's store, then May's Variety). At some point in his life, Trohon fell from staging while doing carpenter work on a church steeple, hitting the ground feet first and shattering his legs. He miraculously recovered but walked thereafter in stiff, springy steps. Digby native Vincent Snow writes of George Trohon in his book *A Treasury of Digby Memories*: "He always took his time cutting hair, telling stories and chatting as he clipped and snipped away. He sometimes practised ventriloquism when standing in back of his customer and working away at hair. All of a sudden a voice would seem to come from the sink in front and he would say, 'Who was that? What did he say?' In the winter time, when the weather was cold, Mr. Trohon would take some kind of hair tonic in his hand and rub it on the back of the head where the hair was missing. His theory was the tonic might keep one from getting cold in the head. There was no extra charge for the tonic and, as I remember it, the price of the cut was twenty-five cents."

JEW COVE

This section of north Water Street near the Government Wharf was known in the late 1800s as Jew Cove. How it came to be named is not known, but it had the reputation then for being somewhat rowdy on Saturday evenings. Tom Farnham of the *Digby Courier* wrote this account in 1948:

In the old days Saturday was not termed a holiday, but it was a sort of "free for all" day. Go to town—stay as long as you like—do as you like—go home when you like—don't care what happens, etc. Remember, I'm not talking about today. It was long, long ago. On Saturday farmers from surrounding villages would come in town with loads of wood, vegetables, lumber, etc. and in turn would take back the value of food and clothing. After all their exchanging was completed, many of the group would retire to some of the "dives" in the Cove, have lunch and refresh themselves— principally refreshments. About sundown the semi-sober members lined up the group, ordered each man to his team and start for home. Those refusing to go were thrown out. Here is where "noisy revelry" started and continued long into the evening. Here is the joke. A very dignified, loyal and sportsmanlike gentleman farmer lived in a house by the railroad crossing near Scotia Restaurant. He was very much annoyed by the frequent disturbance caused by these neighborly young farmers several times a season and often remarked if he knew the ringleaders of the outfit he would give them a thorough "trouncing." Many encouraged the idea and watched the gentleman farmer during the next episode. They found that at the beginning of the fracas he would go to his barn, lock the door, bury himself in the hay near a peek hole, shiver and shake until everything was quiet, then rush out the driveway and ask the first person he met, "What's going on around here; thought I heard a commotion," rolling up his sleeves in the meantime. After being told what happened, throwing his hat on the ground, he said, "Show me the man that started this row and I will give him a thorough trouncing."

JEW COVE

Several private residences and a variety of businesses were situated in Jew Cove, including James Brown's Fish Market, Randolph Dakin's Paint Loft, three buildings owned by Edward Marshall (housing a shoe store, a bakery, and a barbershop), Bill Roop's hotel (later called Short's Hotel), and a Chinese laundry. Featured in this close-up view is a well-known cove businessman Maurice Webber, nicknamed "Cacciac" (holding rolled-up paper), who stands amid sidewalk produce and dry goods with signs advertising Buy Here And Save Money and This is the Cheap Cash Bargain Store.

H.T. WARNE
1868-1952

Hubert Tupper Warne was a fourth-generation descendent of Loyalist Samuel Warne, who moved from the Shelburne Road sometime after 1799 and settled on the outskirts of Digby at Hillgrove. Tupper, better known as "HT" to his friends, grew up on the family homestead; at the age of 15 he left school to work in a Weymouth lumber camp. Exact dates are not available, but after a few years he married and opened a small lumber mill near his home. Hearing of the great timber resources on the west coast, Tupper is said to have rented a railway car around 1900 and moved his family and an entire mill crew to British Columbia where he set up milling operations on a remote lake, the only means of contacting civilization being to flag down a passing train. Tupper returned to Digby a year later, having received word the Hillgrove mill had been experiencing managerial difficulties during his absence. The business flourished under his direction, so much so that a new expansive mill (see below) was built in south-end Digby. In 1903, a three-storey structure known as the Warne Block was

WARNE'S
MILL

erected on Water Street. Built at a cost of $16,000, it housed a grocery store, office space for H.T. Warne Limited, and an apartment where the family first lived before moving into a house on Montague Row. Tupper Warne's varied business interests—which included lumbering and milling operations, pulpwood and pit props, retail sales, and a truck assembly plant—employed hundreds until the 1940s. At the time of his death in 1952, the Warne name had become "well-known in the business life of the province." Daughter-in-law Louise Morse Warne, 97, who still resides at Digby, remembers the respect Tupper commanded among his peers: "Cutting short his education, plus all his years in lumber camps hadn't helped Tupper's ill-use of the English language but strangely enough this seemed to make no difference to several of his well-educated friends (including Dr. Cutten, President of Acadia University). He seemed to have a certain down-to-earth wisdom in his conversation which they appreciated, along with their respect for all he had done on his own."

At least two mills operated in Digby before or around the time of H.T. Warne. In the late 1800s Sydney Wood ran the Digby Manufacturing Company, making lumber, framing, moulding, and fish-packing boxes. Sydney Wood may also have produced wooden piping for the town's first water system in 1895, as he was directly involved in its construction. The Digby Manufacturing Company mill burned in September 1899. R.M. Oliver and A.H. Holdsworth later opened the Digby Woodworking Company c. 1904, manufacturing a complete house-finishing line of doors, sashes, sheathing, and mouldings, with store fixtures advertised as its speciality. S.L. Sullis opened a wooden box factory in 1909 at Digby, described as "a great boon to the packers of boxed fish."

Defiance Truck Agency

With the era of mechanization overtaking the ox and horse, Tupper Warne travelled to Defiance, Ohio in the 1920s and brokered a deal to assemble Defiance trucks at his Digby mill site. A team of American mechanics was brought in to assist Warne's master mechanic Reg Weir in getting the plant up and running. Few details are available concerning this ambitious project, as company records were burned in a 1935 fire that destroyed the Warne Block building. However, many residents still remember the rugged, versatile vehicle dubbed "Warne's Cannonball," so named because their noisy nature allowed them to be heard long before seen. Consumer demand must have been high, for the *Digby Courier* of February 1, 1929 carried the following announcement:

> New Service Building for Defiance Trucks Will Be Erected At Warne Mill. A five thousand dollar concrete building to house the servicing equipment of the Defiance Trucks Agency held by H.T. Warne will be constructed as soon as weather conditions permit....This new building will give Warne's the equipment of servicing an ever growing fleet of Defiance Trucks in operation all over the province and will mean a considerable addition to the pay roll staff. Decision to erect the service plant was reached recently during the visit of Mr. H.T. Warne and Mr. Hubert Warne [son] to Boston, where they met Mr. Nate Robinson, President of the Company which manufactures Defiance Trucks.

The loss of the $50,000 Warne Block in the midst of a Depression no doubt contributed to the demise of the Defiance truck. "Such an achievement in a little town the size of Digby," writes daughter-in-law Louise Morse Warne, "caused both amazement and jubilation in all but the company office where the figures showed that it had come at too high a cost. Production continued for a time...but eventually they had to face the fact it was too large an enterprise for too small an area. Thus the Defiance truck became history with the reputation of being a mechanical success but a financial failure. Unfortunate as this may have been, for those closely involved with the project, there was not so much a sense of failure as a faint glow of satisfaction in having proved that it could be done."

WARNE'S MOBILE 'DEFIANCE' GROCERY

Warne's operated this mobile grocery to service the many communities scattered throughout Digby County. Hubert and Dora Warne, Tupper's children and business partners, took a more active role in the daily running of the company as their father grew older and began showing the early signs of Alzheimers. Despite closure of the Defiance assembly plant, and the loss of the Warne Block building in the 1930s the box factory, pulpwood exports, and the wartime contract for ammunition boxes managed to keep the company afloat for a few more years. Hubert Warne (1902-1980) was a member of the committee that, in 1943, successfully lobbied Ottawa to build the naval training base H.M.C.S. Cornwallis, just ten miles from Digby. However, what was hoped would be salvation for H.T. Warne turned out to be its death knell. Already committed to a signed contract for manufacturing ammunition boxes at a set price, Hubert Warne could not match the higher government wages paid to workers to build Cornwallis. Despite promises from Ottawa of a subsidy to offset losses, none was forthcoming, and financial ruin was close at hand. In stepped a banker by the name of Vanderwald, who is said to have escaped to Canada ahead of Hitler's take-over of Germany. Under the guise of friendship, loans were forthcoming and as company debts piled up Vanderwald became more "helpful," filling staff vacancies at Warne's with his own employees. This eventually amounted to a corporate take-over, as Vanderwald was principally involved in pulpwood and wanted Warne's timber resources. As is alleged to have happened to mills in Weymouth and New Brunswick around the same time, Vanderwald assumed control through bankrupcy proceedings, then closed all operations while retaining deeds to any lands. Fortunately, perhaps, for Tupper Warne, his debilitating disease allowed him to finish his days unmindful of the events surrounding the loss of his life's work.

Delivering ice

The cutting, transporting, and storage of ice was an annual winter event. In 1906 G.H. McCormick built a bait freezer and icehouse in south-end Digby, in connection with his large clam business. The freezer closed after a short time, but in 1923 was converted into the Jack & Cardoza jam factory. When this failed in the 1930s, some of the space became a bunkhouse for H.T. Warne employees. In this January 30, 1929 photo, E.H. Raymond's Defiance truck makes an ice delivery to Maritime Fish Corporation from William Franklin's ice pond in Conway. The picture was printed in the *Digby Courier* because the Defiance was only built to carry 2 1/2 tons, but on this occasion was loaded with over twice that weight. The article went on to report that Raymond's truck delivered more than 62 tons on that particular day. With so much focus on the fresh fishery, great quantities of ice were required in Digby and in surrounding communities. A vessel would normally carry 25 tons of block ice; in the years before mechanization, this came "from the country back of the town and through the medium of painfully slow ox-drawn wagons." Upon arrival at the docks, the ice would be hoisted aboard using block and tackle suspended from the rigging, then stowed in the vessel's hold. Icing the catch was a labour-intensive process in itself, as the ice had to be first broken down into small pieces in fish pens below decks. Crew members used iron draw knives to shave down the blocks, working by the light of "sticking tommies"—pointed metal candleholders that were sharpened at both ends and driven into the ship's bulkhead. Mild winters in the early 1950s threatened the local fishing trade with a shortage of ice. As a result, businessmen Clayton and Vincent Snow, Urbain Belliveau, Greg Gilliatt—with the backing of 25 shareholders—purchased ice-making machinery and formed the Digby County Ice Company. This business consortium serviced the area for years, until individual fish plants began installing their own ice-making equipment, at which time the Digby County Ice Company was sold to the fishing firm C.D. Snow (later owned by O'Neil Fisheries of Digby).

Chapter 3

Public &
Professional Service

EXCAVATING THE WATER RESERVOIR

Workmen pause from digging a water reservoir near Sydney Street for this early 1890s photo. Plans for a town water system began in 1892, when two competing companies submitted proposals to town council, but it was not until April 1895 that work actually began. Council had decided to install the water works itself, rather than contracting privately, and $35,000 was alotted for the project. Sydney Wood of Digby and G.A. Vye of Bridgeville (who later became Digby's Superintendent of Streets and Water) tendered a successful construction bid; a local contractor offered to supply cheap Italian labor but Sydney Wood declined, choosing instead "to patronize local industry." Within eight months, Digby had 8 miles of pipe line, 19 fire hydrants, a masonry dam holding 11 million gallons of water and a 600,000-gallon reservoir. The drinking water, although noticeably discoloured, was deemed "excellent...and expected to clear up shortly."

Rev. Edward William Brudenell, chaplain of Admiral Digby's warship *Atalanta* reportedly "preached the first sermon in 1783 ever delivered at Digby." He was followed by Reverend Jacob Bailey, Rector of Annapolis Royal, who preached at Digby on September 11, 1785. Early

on, meetings were held in settlers' homes. The first recorded marriage at Digby took place on June 22, 1786, when Mento LeSage wed Rachel Bell, widow of Captain Jeremiah Bell, in a ceremony conducted by Reverend Brudenell. Digby Trinity Parish began on Michaelmas Day, 1785, when a number of Loyalists (who had been members of New York's Anglican Trinity Parish) held a Vestry Meeting to elect church officers. Parish boundaries were established by Governor Parr in 1786; on August 28, Reverend Roger Viets (from Connecticut) was inducted as the first Rector. Two Anglican churches have stood on the Queen Street site, the original cornerstone laid in 1788 by Nova Scotia's first Bishop, Rt. Reverend Charles Inglis, who had been rector to many of the parishoners before their move to Digby. An interesting note was the assignment of pews. "To prevent jealousy and confusion no pew is to be assigned to any person but by auction to the highest bidder. There is to be a certain number of pews left for free pews—also there is to be pews left for negro pews in the back of the church, also the christening pew, the minister's pew and a pew for strange gentlemen." In 1817, any pew holder failing to attend church at least once a month had his pew forfeited and sold. By 1874, all pews were free. Shipbuilder Martin Oliver began work on a new church in 1878 (pictured here) from plans drawn by well-known New England architect Stephen Earle. The new Trinity was consecrated October 15, 1880, with seating for 750 parishoners. Notable members included Admiral Robert Digby, who maintained a reserved pew with his coat of arms emblazened upon the door; Thomas C. Sherve, the town's first mayor from 1890-92; John Edison, Thomas Edison's great-grandfather; and Lieutenant James Foreman, reputedly the founder of North America's first Sunday school.

Enroute to Yarmouth in 1791, Reverend Joseph Dimock stopped at Weymouth and preached a sermon, which, according to Isaiah Wilson, "probably was the advent of Baptist Missions in the County." Six years later, Reverend Enoch Towner,

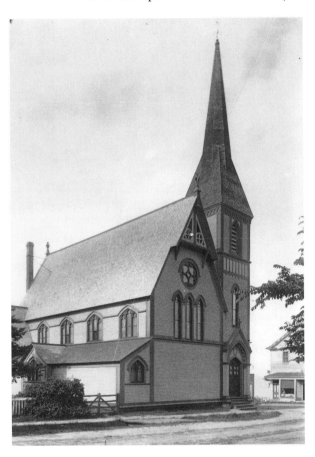

a recent Episcopalian convert to the New Light or Baptist Church at Lower Granville, preached at settlements throughout Digby County at which time "there was not a single adherent of the sect among its inhabitants." However, by the early 1800s, Reverend Towner and "his Lieutenant" Peter Crandall had attracted more than two hundred Baptist followers, "the most flourishing sect during the first four decades of this century." In 1809, Crandall preached the first Baptist sermon at Digby in the home of a widow McDormand. During the service, which was attended by a large congregation, "the less orderly [who] were unwilling to allow this innovation on the Established faith, hitherto undisturbed by Baptist aggression" broke windows and demanded the meeting end; local constabulary had to restore order. The result was a 28-year hiatus for the Digby Baptists until Reverend Joseph Crandall, brother of Peter Crandall, arrived from New Brunswick on Sunday July 2, 1837, to preach in a vacated house. He later baptized William L. Bent, M.D. and his sister, Mrs. Phineas Lovett, Jr. in the Annapolis Basin, which "was the earliest immersion performed in the town, and was witnessed by an immense concourse." On September 30, 1839, the Digby Baptist Church was organized with Reverend Samuel Bancroft as pastor. A small church building completed in 1842 on Queen Street between Mount and Church Streets ministered to residents of Digby, Broad Cove (Culloden), and Digby Neck as far as Hutchinson's Brook.

The Digby Baptists later moved into the church pictured here, still in use today. This structure was built c. 1876 first as a Reformed Episcopal Church by disgruntled members of Digby's Trinity Parish. The short-lived movement ironically chose for its site that of pre-Loyalist William McDormand's property from which Reverend Peter Crandall had been driven many years earlier after Digby's first Baptist sermon. Presbyterians later used this church until it was purchased by Baptists.

ST. PATRICK'S ROMAN CATHOLIC CHAPEL

St. Patrick's Roman Catholic Chapel was built by Irish immigrants in 1834 on the corner of King and Prince William Streets. For a hundred years the small edifice, pictured here, served the town's Catholic congregation, until ground was broken for a new and larger church in 1934, near Queen Street. For the next seven years, the Catholic congregation worshiped in the Oddfellows Hall on Water Street, or in the basement of the unfinished church, until the building was finally completed in 1941. Their first service in the new church was held on Sunday, August 10, 1941.

The Catholics "disseminated their doctrines among the Indians long before the Protestants were sufficiently numerous to organize and erect churches." In 1767, the Township of Clare was established along St. Mary's Bay. Later known as the French Shore, this area was set aside for repatriated Acadians whose original farm lands had been taken in the years after their 1755 expulsion. The first Acadiens began returning in 1768, "uneducated and without capital, they toiled, and eventually gathered abundant harvests in provisions, clothing and other necessaries." In 1770, Pére Charles François Bailly de Messeir arrived at Clare and within the year established "the Premier Church built in Digby County for the worship of Almighty God." Some among the Acadians were "elementary scholars" but, for the most part, "educational facilities were almost unknown to the citizens." Conditions improved dramatically with the arrival of Abbé John M. Sigogne in 1799 when he began teaching religious studies and rudimentary education at Grosses Coques as well as acting as legal and political advisor to the Acadians. Revered by his parishioners, Abbé Sigogne—"undoubtedly the principal character in French Acadian history in Nova Scotia"—ministered in Clare, Tusket, and Pubnico until his death in 1844. The earliest "lay" teacher of record was a M. Brunelle, who arrived from France around 1825 and taught at Clare for a number of years. The Catholic influence along the French Shore is evident in the establishment of the Chicaben Academy at Church Point c. 1857, the Convent of Sacred Hearts at Meteghan, and, in 1890, the College Sainte-Anne at Church Point.

DISCIPLES OF CHRIST CHURCH, c. 1902

The Disciples of Christ, known also as Campbellites, came to Digby County in 1852, when Donald Crawford visited Southville and formed an 11-member church. Not overly popular during its brief history only five churches had been erected by 1876 at Southville, Briar Island, Tiverton, Gulliver's Cove and South Range. Reverend H.A. Devoe, who ministered at Southville, was responsible in 1902 for establishing a Disciples of Christ Church on Sydney Street in Digby. Over two-thirds of its three-thousand-dollar construction cost was donated by the Reverend Devoe, who also designed the building. The interior of the church featured walls and ceiling of hardwood sheathing, and 12 gothic leaded glass windows; Digby Woodworking Company manufactured 46 rows of circular pews, which seated 350 worshipers. When the church closed c. 1920, many in the congregation joined Grace Methodist, and eventually Carl Eldridge bought the building for a private residence.

The house with double verandahs featured to the left of the church sits at 152 Queen Street and belonged to George Vye, the Superintendent of Streets for Digby. He and his wife owned and operated Vye's Café at the old railway station on First Avenue. The grand residence to the right at 158 Queen Street belonged to Major John Daley, a prominant Digby resident who fought in the Boer War, owned the Digby Power Plant, published The *Digby Weekly Courier* for a time and served as Lieutenant Governor of Nova Scotia. An avid hunter and outdoorsman, Major Daley was also instrumental in the re-introduction of white-tail deer to the province in the mid-1890s. An interesting feature of his home was its granite foundation, the stones ferried ten miles by barge from Bear River. The landscaped property was noted for its archway, built from the jawbone of an albino whale shot in the Annapolis Basin, by Major Daley, from a canoe. The jawbone arch, topped by a set of moose antlers, served as a gateway to the property and for many years was a popular Digby landmark.

GRACE (METHODIST) UNITED CHURCH, PRINCE WILLIAM STREET

In 1785, Digby was visited by Freeborn Garretson, an American Methodist evangelist, and William Black, the "father" of Maritime Methodism. It was through their efforts that a Methodist Society was organized in the summer of 1786 at the Black community of Brindley Town on the outskirts of Digby. Of the society's 78 members, 66 were Black. When the majority of Blacks left Digby for Sierra Leone in 1792 a period of stagnation set in for the Methodists until 1819, when a Methodist chapel was built on the site of the present United Church parsonage. For many years "Methodism was considered not so much a separate denomination but a movement within the established church" and as such the services of the Anglican rector were used for marriages, baptisms, and funerals. Methodism died out again in the 1820s but was revived in 1831 with the arrival of preachers Michael Pickles and William Marshall. Pickles was instrumental in having work completed on the partially-finished chapel, while Marshall started Digby's first temperance society. These men were followed in 1851 by Reverend James Taylor, who preached a circuit that included Digby, Brighton, and Barton (known then as St. Mary's Bay), Weymouth, Sandy Cove, Westport, Trout Cove (Centreville), Broad Cove, Bloomfield Settlement, and North Range. The years between 1860 and 1895 were a period of growth for Digby Methodists; a new church (pictured here) opened in 1860, and the original chapel was moved to the corner of Sydney Street and First Avenue, where it was used as a stable and carriage shop until it burnt in the fire of 1899. The Methodist church steeple, which served to guide ships into the harbour, blew off in 1878; it was replaced that same year when the church was sawn in half and enlarged. Rededicated on December 13, 1880, a church hall (left) was built in 1884 and a new parsonage in 1900. Now featuring a 'wedding cake' top in place of its steeple, Grace Methodist Church became part of the new United Church of Canada in 1925, when a religious and economic union brought together most of those from the Congregational, Presbyterian and Methodist faiths.

STAGE COACH TALLYHOO, WATER STREET, C. 1890

The earliest record of stage coach travel in Digby County dates to 1844 when a semi-weekly service carrying mail and passengers opened between Digby and Yarmouth. Accounts are sketchy, but in the late 1870s it is known that George Stailing and Son of Digby owned stables in the vicinity of the Digby House on Queen Street and the railroad tracks on First Avenue. Here in these stables—which encompassed an entire town block—he kept ten horses and four Dalmatians, the latter used as protection against highwaymen. Depending upon road conditions, as many as four horses would be used to pull the coach. Passengers embarked for the trip aboard the Tallyhoo Stage on Water Street in front of the *Digby Courier* and Royal Hotel buildings as featured in this photo. When all was readied, driver Fred Cousins would begin the first 20 mile leg of the journey to Weymouth with the coach dogs running along, tied to the rear of the stage. At Jones's Hotel and Stables in Weymouth, an exchange of mail and passengers would be made, meals served, the horses and dogs rested and the reins passed to Weymouth native Bob Newcombe and his assistant, Joe Horne from Digby. Around midnight the stage left for Meteghan, where it stopped at Ed Sheehan's Royal Hotel. Following a similar routine here as before, the coach was driven to Yarmouth by Charlie Hutchins of Digby. The return 70-mile trip began the following day, making sailing connections at Digby with steamers bound for Annapolis Royal or Saint John, N.B.

Around the same era as the Digby-Yarmouth run, another stage coach under contract to W.H. Eldridge of Sandy Cove operated from Digby to Digby Neck and the Islands. Leaving Digby at 4:00 P.M., the 45-mile "express service" stopped at all way offices until reaching East Ferry. Mail and passengers would then be conveyed on 'By' Blackford's ferry across Petite Passage to Long Island's Tiverton, where Ned Blackford carried on to Central Grove and Freeport. At Grand Passage, Ralph Morrell's ferry completed the trip to Westport on Brier Island.

DIGBY RAILWAY STATION, C. 1891

This steam locomotive bearing the inscription "Weymouth" on its side and a prominent #8 on the front was built in 1879 by the Portland Company of Portland, Maine. That same year, Weymouth #8 was delivered to the Western Counties Railway, which was building a line between Yarmouth and Annapolis Royal. It served until the Canadian Pacific Railway—which by 1912 controlled local operations—began modernizing locomotive and steamship services c. 1920.

The original Digby Station pictured here—which narrowly escaped burning in the Fire of 1899—played an integral role in Digby's early telegraph system. The Nova Scotia Telegraph Company was incorporated at Halifax in 1851, and soon opened offices in "principal towns" throughout the province. In 1860, the

American Telegraph Company leased all lines in Nova Scotia, but was subsequently replaced by the Western Union Telegraph Company from New York, which first leased, then purchased, all the Maritime lines. Digby's telegraph office opened on December 3, 1855 on the second floor of Edward Marshall's store on Water Street, with John Robinson as its first operator. He was succeeded by his son Charles B. Robinson in 1857, who was replaced by Miss Mary E. Smyth in 1859; Smyth was replaced by William B. Stewart in 1863, who served until the coming of the railway in the 1870s. With its completion, the Station Agent then assumed the duties as "ex-officio operator" of the telegraph.

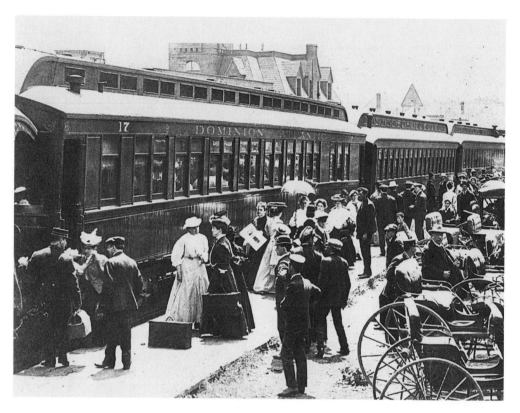

A BUSY DAY AT THE TRAIN STATION, C. 1900

The building of the Western Counties Railway through Digby County in the 1870s was controversial. Coastal towns favoured a shore route while lumbering communities from the interior pressed for the route to run farther inland. A compromise was reached in 1872, whereby the rail lines would follow an interior route from Yarmouth to Weymouth, then out to the coast until reaching Annapolis Royal. The Yarmouth to Annapolis Royal branch (which then would continue on via Windsor & Annapolis Railway) was to be 93 miles in length and divided into 13 sections. Work on the Yarmouth-Digby line began in September 1873, and on September 29, 1879 it opened for business. Unfortunately, the Western Counties Railway had run out of money, leaving a 22-mile unfinished gap between Digby and Annapolis Royal. This "Missing Link" made it necessary for a passenger travelling between Halifax and Yarmouth to make numerous transfers to complete the 217-mile trip. In the confusing world of railway builders and running rights, from Halifax to Windsor-Junction one rode the Intercolonial Railway, then from Windsor Junction to Windsor, transfer was made to the Western Counties Railway. From Windsor the weary traveller next took the Windsor & Annapolis Railway to Annapolis Royal. At Annapolis Royal the switch was made to a stagecoach or coastal steamer for the trip around the "missing link" to Digby where connections were again made with the Western Counties Railway for the final leg of the journey to Yarmouth.

PART OF THE "MISSING LINK"

An early 1900s postcard depicts the train trestle (left) and Victoria Bridge, which spanned the mouth of Bear River separating Digby and Annapolis Counties. Both of these bridges swung open to allow vessels access to the village of Bear River three miles upstream. This point of the river was known as "Halibut Eddy" and was crossed by means of a ferry, before the one lane Victoria Bridge was built in 1865. Solomon Maillet started the ferry service at the turn of the nineteenth century, charging a fare of sixpence, sterling. It was taken over for a short time by a Mr. Pine from Clements before Captain Isaac Winchester and his brother Spencer assumed duties c. 1805; they were followed by Isaac's son Charles Winchester Sr. (1813-1927). The Victoria Bridge, which was rebuilt c. 1886-91, was once the longest vehicular bridge in Nova Scotia.

A major hurdle in completing the missing railway link between Digby and Annapolis were the train trestles required to bridge the Grand Joggin, Bear River and Moose River. In 1891 the Dominion Government intervened and "as a public service" spent $1 million to finish the Digby-Annapolis Royal section. In 1893 the Western Counties Railway was reorganized as the Yarmouth and Annapolis Railway. Due to financial losses, it was sold in 1894 to the Windsor & Annapolis Railway, which, by an act of Federal Parliament, became the Dominion Atlantic Railway that same year. On October 1, 1894 the first through train made the Halifax-Yarmouth run in nine hours. The Dominion Atlantic Railway (DAR) continued operations until 1911 when Canadian Pacific Railway leased all DAR facilities (except the Yarmouth steamship business which DAR also owned) for 999 years. The "Dominion Atlantic Railway" name was retained, but it was controlled by Canadian Pacific Railway. Today, only a few reminants remain from the days of the silver rails, such as the rusting Bear River trestle, which stands as mute testament to a lost era.

STEAM PACKET *BEAR RIVER*

"Packets" were small vessels used for conveying freight, mail, and passengers between coastal ports. Sail-driven packets ferried between Saint John, Digby and Annapolis from the earliest settlement of Loyalists. These were the *Sally*, captained first by Jeremiah Bell, then by John Beyea; the *Mary Ann*, captained by Robert Turnbull; and the *Matilda*, owned by James and Charles Thomas of Saint John. When the *Matilda* ceased operating in about 1814, the sloop *Hairm*, owned by William Taylor and commanded by a Captain Wiley, continued the packet service until the arrival of steamers in the early 1800s. In this c. 1919 photo, the steam packet *Bear River*, carrying a deckload of apples bound for Saint John, N.B., waits at the mouth of Bear River for the swing section of the railroad trestle to be opened. Built in 1905 at Shelburne, N.S. the *Bear River* plied her trade until the 1930s, also providing towage service in the Annapolis Basin. Over the years, various steam-driven packets maintained weekly connections with Bear River, Annapolis, Digby, Goat Island, Port Wade, Smith's Cove and Victoria Beach, until the service was discontinued shortly after the outbreak of World War II.

PADDLE WHEELER *MONTICELLO* LEAVING DIGBY PIER

The first steamer to cross the Bay of Fundy from Saint John to Digby and Annapolis was the small 87-ton paddle wheeler *St. John*, built in 1826 at Deer Island, N.B. After its initial season of 1827, the vessel was purchased by James Whitney of Saint John, who began a 30-year ferry service on the Fundy run. Around 1836, fares were as follows: Saint John to Digby in summer $1.50, in winter $2.00; Saint John to Annapolis Royal in summer $2.00, in winter $2.50. By 1841 steamers of 250 tons were sailing the Saint John, Digby, Annapolis Royal route on a bi-weekly schedule, which increased to three round trips a week within ten years.

Competing firms and a succession of improved steamers helped ferry operations develop rapidly and by the 1880s Digby, Annapolis Royal, Windsor and Yarmouth were well served with inter-connecting routes to Saint John, Portland, Boston and New York. In 1885 a tourist could purchase a one-way fare for $5.25 from Boston to Digby via Saint John, N.B. The Bay of Fundy Steamship Company was incorporated in January 1889 and immediately placed the steam paddle-wheeler *City of Monticello* (pictured here) on the Fundy route between Saint John and Digby. Sold in 1899 and switched to the Yarmouth-Saint John run, she sank in rough weather on November 10, 1900 off Cape Forchu near Yarmouth, resulting in the deaths of 36 passengers and crew.

Until the late 1800s, Annapolis Royal—not Digby—was the terminal point on the Saint John-Digby-Annapolis Royal route. This changed in 1891 with the completion of the "Missing Link" and the creation, three years later, of the Dominion Atlantic Railway. From that day until the present, Digby has been the Nova Scotia port-of-call for the Bay of Fundy ferry.

S.S. *Empress* (LEFT), S.S. *Princess Helene* at Digby Pier, 1930

In 1895 the newly-formed Dominion Atlantic Railway purchased the 1125-ton, 21-knot steam paddlewheeler S.S. *Prince Rupert* and placed her on the Saint John-Digby run in direct competition to the Bay of Fundy Steamship Company's slower, aging *Monticello*. Unable to keep pace, the *Monticello* was sold in 1899 to the Yarmouth Steamship Company, and the Bay of Fundy Steamship Company closed its operations. The DAR then turned a monopolistic eye to the Yarmouth-Boston route. The Yarmouth S.S. Company had been battling since 1897 to survive. In 1899, the DAR began operating the steamships *Prince Edward, Prince George* and *Prince Arthur* to challenge the S.S. *Yarmouth* and S.S. *Boston* for business. A price war ensued and DAR prevailed, buying out the Yarmouth S.S. in June 1901. Over the next decade a whirlwind of activity followed, with rumours of a Canadian Pacific Railway take-over of DAR, competition on the homefront from American shipping firms, and a continual changing of ferries servicing the Saint John-Digby and Yarmouth-Boston routes. When the dust settled in 1912, the American-based Eastern S.S. Corporation controlled the Yarmouth-Boston run, with DAR retaining the Bay of Fundy. A year later, Canadian Pacific took control of the Saint John-Digby ferry, leaving DAR with railway operations. In 1916, the S.S. *Empress*, out-fitted with electricity and driven by twin-screws and 365-horsepower engines began ferrying the Fundy waters. After 14 years of storm-tossed crossings, and lacking the capability to accomodate automobiles, she was replaced on August 29, 1930 by the *Princess Helene*. This photo shows the size discrepancy of the two vessels, the *Princess Helene* equipped to carry five hundred passengers, fifty automobiles, and double the freight of her predecessor.

NEW DIGBY PIER, 1931

The February 13, 1931 issue of the *Digby Courier* carried the following announcement:

The completion of the new pier at Digby for the Canadian Pacific S.S. *Princess Helene* has been an important factor in enabling the DAR-CPR service to reduce freight schedules by 48 hours between N.S. points and points Montreal and West. The new schedule provides for a three day package freight delivery to Montreal, 4 days to Toronto from points on the Dominion Atlantic lines, with an equally fast schedule on incoming or eastern bound freight....New methods and electric elevators at the Digby pier have made it possible to handle easily all through freight in the limited time available, establishing a fast dependable service over this route.... The Dominion Atlantic Railway is to be congratulated upon thus further improving the service over the Valley route which is becoming increasingly popular for through shipments. The increased activity cannot fail but react upon the general prosperity and progress of the Valley.

The retired *Empress* was gutted by fire in 1931 while moored at Saint John. She was then sold to Dominion Steel and Coal Company and used as a coal barge in Saint John Harbour until scrapped. The *Princess Helene* survived the U-boat infested Bay of Fundy during World War II, and two strikes by the railway and Seafarers International Union. On April 27, 1963, the *Princess* was relieved of her duties after 33 years of service. She was subsequently sold to a business group in Athens, Greece and used as a cruise ship in the Mediterranean. Her replacement was the *Princess of Nanaimo*, a west-coast-based vessel weighing 6,800 tons with carrying capacity for 1,000 passengers and 120 automobiles. Renamed the *Princess of Acadia*, she made her first run on April 29, 1963. Her tour of duty, however, was brief. To meet the increased demands of modern freight transportation, a *Princess of Acadia II* began operations on June 1, 1971, which had the capability of ferrying 650 passengers, along with 159 automobiles or 40 tractor-trailer trucks. A $16 million government-funded docking facility was built two miles from Digby on Shore Road. While the old terminal and parts of the wharf were demolished long ago, a two hundred–year-old service continues today.

The first capital crime in Digby County was committed on July 17, 1786, when "Purdy, a constable, (was) killed by one Ott with a musket; a most plain, daring and wilful murder; most provoked and premeditated." Records indicate that constable Daniel Purdy was killed in the line of duty while "quelling a drunken riot." Jacob Ott was subsequently hanged at Annapolis for his crime "while the tavern keeper who furnished the liquor, sitting as foreman of the jury, that condemned him, posed as a leading gentleman of Digby."

For the most part Digby was a peaceful community, its police duties focused on escorting prisoners to court from the neigbouring lock-up, investigating crimes of a relative minor nature, and maintaining a lawful presence. The town police log books for the 1920s show an almost daily verbatim closing entry: "All duties required of me performed. Peace and Order good throughout the day...." Fred J. Thibault policed the streets in the 1930s, working twelve-hour days (on call for the other twelve hours), seven days a week, for an annual salary of $1,000 to $1,200 a year. Guy Dunn was appointed sheriff in January 1943, after having served seven years as deputy. Before retiring in 1968 (when he was succeeded by his son Webster), Guy averaged up to fifteen thousand miles a year travelling through the county, generally dealing with matters of a civil nature, serving warrants and summons. During his 25 years, he also made many trips to New Brunswick's Dorchester Penitentiary, escorting prisoners.

SHERIFF H.A.P. SMITH

Henry Albert Patterson Smith, better known as H.A.P. Smith, has been described as "one of the more colourful characters Nova Scotia has ever produced." He was born in Digby on April 24, 1864, the son of Dr. Peleg Wiswell Smith and Sarah Eliza (nee Viets). H.A.P. Smith was a man of many parts—High Sheriff of Digby County, game warden, founding father of the Nova Scotia Guides Association, acknowledged ornithologist, avid cricket player, skilled marksman and fisherman, dog breeder, and published author.

Smith's passion was the out-of-doors, his services as a professional wilderness guide widely sought among visiting American sportsmen. His demonstrations of marksmanship were legendary; at a guides meet at Yarmouth in the early 1900s, Smith dazzled spectators with his rifle by clipping the ashes off a cigarette held in a man's mouth. He followed this by shooting the brass casings off five empty shotgun shells on a volunteer's fingertips, then proceeded to take a pump-action .22 and—firing a shot into the air—pumped another round into the chamber and fired again, knocking the spent shell casing out of mid-air; he repeated this 20 times in rapid succession without a miss. As Digby's sheriff, it's little wonder that he had "the reputation of being able to go into lumber camps, on board ships where there was trouble, and in among a lot of hostile people, and go alone."

H.A.P. Smith is today "regarded as the first publicist of Nova Scotia's tolling retrievers" and on numerous occasions wrote passionately of the duck toller's distinct qualities in the leading outdoor journals of the time, including *Forest & Stream*. He also figured prominately in the 1894 re-introduction of white-tail deer into Nova Scotia, introduced to replace the declining moose population and the soon-to-be extinct caribou. Henry Albert Patterson Smith died at Saint John, N.B. on April 23, 1923.

Digby's first courthouse was built in 1838 just off Queen Street. After 70 years of service, a new one (featured here) was constructed c. 1908 on the same site. This impressive Queen Ann Revival structure, still used today, cost the then-princely sum of $40,000 and included a new jail that not only provided housing for the criminal element but more commodious accomodations for the jailer and his family.

Hangings were not a common practice, but two celebrated cases are attached to Digby. On December 16, 1875 a man by the name of Robbins met his end at the county lockup for "the wilful murder of his wife." Having first shot her with a rifle while she slept, then bludgeoning her with a mallet, Robbins avoided arrest for 11 days while hiding out in the woods. During this time he emerged at night to harass his wife's family—torching their barns, shaving the tails of their horses and leaving death threats. He was finally captured while sleeping by his campfire and escorted in shackles to Digby. The story goes that when apprehended, his hair was jet-black but that on the day of his execution a short time later it had turned snow white.

A more infamous case was the death of Annie Kempton from Bear River, who, in January, 1896 "was murdered in her father's house in a desperate struggle to preserve her chastity." A drifter by the name of Peter Wheeler was subsequently arrested, convicted, and sentenced to be hanged at Digby on September 8, 1896. Hundreds gathered to witness the event on the day prior to execution. With excitement and anger running high, a substantially large vigilante force was poised to extract their own punishment by lynching Wheeler. Getting wind of their intentions, Sheriff VanBlarcom carried out the sentence at 2:35A.M. instead of the scheduled time of daybreak, thereby avoiding "the arrest and trial of some of the ringleaders in the Supreme Court, for wilful murder." The last person hanged at Digby is said to have been the murderer John Thibault in August, 1912.

NEW COUNTY LOCKUP

CLASS PHOTO OF MISS BELLE REDDING AND STUDENTS

From Isaiah Wilson's county history we learn that "when the pioneers located in Conway (Digby), they provided educational advantages for their children. Though living somewhat isolated from each other, a worthy and competent tutor formed one of their number. William Barbancks went daily from one habitation to another, teaching each family the inestimable blessings of reading, writing and arithmetic." Barbancks left Digby after a short time and taught for many years in the county at Gulliver's Cove, Waterford, Sandy Cove, Little River, Tiverton, Freeport, Brier Island, Marshalltown, Grand Joggin, and Smith's Cove. He is credited with being "the earliest teacher who pursued this important calling in the County," serving an entire settlement on some occasions, at other times teaching only one or two families.

When William Barbancks left Digby, Lieutenant James Foreman, "a faithful, experienced and efficient Graduate of a High School in England" opened a town school in the front room of his home in November, 1784, which was attended by 75 students for an eight month term. During the summers of 1785 and 1786, he also taught the equivalent of Sunday School for those of the Anglican faith. However, Foreman's home school was soon found to be inconveniently located, cold and lacking adequate furnishings, and in 1789 volunteers erected a school building in Block X, facing an alley between Water and Queen Streets. Of modest size, it was outfitted with a brick furnace and extension desks, the older students seated along the walls and elementary ages arranged at the centre. This school served Digby until the Compulsory Education Act in 1864, when an Academy was built on the corner of Church and Queen Streets. By 1897 there were 106 schools in Digby County.

Jessie Turnbull (nee Titus) poses c. 1905 with her three sons: (left to right) John Fulton, George Archer, and Guy Victor. Before marrying in 1893, Jessie taught school from about 1886 to 1892 in the "Intermediate Department" (grades 5-7) at the Digby Academy, then transfered briefly to the "Preparatory Department." Personal diary entries indicate she was a popular teacher:

WED. OCT. 26, 1892 - *My scholars presented me with a glove box, handkerchief and bottle of perfume, vase.*

FRI. OCT 28, 1892 - *My last day of school. Winnie gave me a fruit basket and in the afternoon some of my scholars gave me an epergne (dinner table centre piece). My scholars kissed me Good-bye.*

A footnote to Jessie's school teaching career was the publication in 1893 of her small booklet, "Insects of Nova Scotia." It received glowing reviews, and was recommended reading by L.S. Morse, Inspector of Schools: "Teachers will find these notes, the basis of which is largely the result of original investigation, of much assistance in preparing and giving oral lessons on this interesting branch of natural science. The small price of the pamphlet (20 cents) will bring it within the reach of all our teachers. I hope, therefore, that it may have a wide circulation, and that it may be the means of bringing the oral lessons on nature required by the course of study into greater prominence in our schools." Superintendent of Education A.H. MacKay wrote: "...When visiting the Digby Academy I had the pleasure of seeing the creditable collections made by yourself and your pupils, as well as other evidence of your study of the natural objects themselves as found within the bounds of your School Section....Your little treatise may be better than a more pretentious work to show our teachers what they can do themselves if they only try."

New Digby Academy, c. 1892

A new brick school was built adjacent to the court house on Queen Street in 1891 to replace the earlier wooden Academy. The old Academy building was sold to the Digby Agricultural Society in 1894 for $40 and was still standing in 1907. The new Academy, which opened in 1892 with two hundred students, had by 1916 grown to three hundred students, seven teachers, and a yearly operating cost of $3,882 to the town. Originally designed with seven classrooms, library, labratory and assembly hall, renovations in 1937 added two classrooms and an auditorium because the student population had doubled. A Rural High School, reportedly the first of its kind in Nova Scotia, opened in 1948; its name was changed in 1955 to the Digby Regional High School. The Academy, which sits vacant today, then became the Primary-Elementary, housing 636 students in 1957. An interesting closing note was the retirement in 1905 of Miss Mary Smallie: after 40 years and three months "of continuous service in Digby schools" teaching advanced primary "not a single record is to be found of dissatisfaction with the teacher or any complaint...."

DIGBY COURIER OFFICE, WATER STREET

David A. Nicholson, a deaf man, was the first to attempt publishing a Digby newspaper in 1857, but his *Weekly Athenaeum* "proved a failure for want of patronage." Two years later, Albert E. Dodge of Annapolis Royal and Ingraham B. Gidney (son of Angus Gidney from Sandy Cove, a former editor of the *Yarmouth Herald*) launched the eight page weekly *Acadian* from their Water Street office. Its motto was "Mind with mind direct communion holds." Yearly subscriptions sold for $2.50 ($2.00 if paid within six months) with first-time advertisement charges of 80 cents and 25 cents thereafter. The *Acadian* "was not a flattering success" and ceased publication in 1862 when the building burned. John A. Cossett & Son were the next to print a local newspaper in 1865 with their four-page *Weekly Examiner*, "a Journal of Art, Science, Literature and General Information." Its time, too, was short lived, and it went out of circulation two years later. Digby was without a newspaper from 1867 until September 18, 1874 when Richard S. McCormick published the first issue of the *Digby Weekly Courier* at $1.50 per annum. He was succeeded by Charles E. Farnham, W.T. Ford, Aubrey Fullerton, Oakes Dunham, George E. Chisholm, John James Wallis, and Edith Wallis. John James Wallis has been called "the Dean of Nova Scotia Weekly Newspapers" beginning his career in 1888 as a printer in the village of Salem near Yarmouth, N.S. He then worked 25 years at the *Yarmouth Times*, eventually rising to managing editor. Wallis moved on to managing and editorial posts with weekly newspapers in Bridgetown, Lunenburg, and Weymouth before taking on the editorship in 1918 of the *Digby Courier*. He held this position until 1924, when he left to establish Wallis Print; he returned in 1931 to become its owner, printer, and editor. When his son and business partner J.M. Wallis died in 1949, daughter-in-law Edith M. (Corkum) Wallis became an Associate Editor, moving to manager and editor in 1955 at the time of J.J. Wallis's death. Now printed by Kentville Publishing in New Minas, N.S., the *Digby Courier*—with an editorial office on Water Street, Digby town—is in its 126th year of reporting local and county news.

INTERIOR OF *DIGBY COURIER* OFFICE

The *Digby Courier* at its outset was politically non-partisan but this changed in 1887 when "it became an exponent of Liberal principles." In response, the Canadian Printing and Publishing Company took up residency in 1891 on the east side of Water Street in the Red Raven building, and began circulating the *Canadian*, a four page tabloid promoting the Conservative party. "A lively warfare of words with a thorough canvass for subscribers now commenced." The battle was short-lived as limited readership would not support two newspapers. When the *Courier* "again donned political independence," the *Canadian*, in 1893, went out of business.

A number of newspapers came and went in Digby County. In 1887 Valentine Landry launched *L'Évangeline* at Digby for the county's substantial Acadien population. In 1888, the first issue of the *Weymouth Times*, "devoted to General News, Literature and County Interests" was published at Weymouth Bridge. One year later it was purchased by *L'Évangeline*, which had moved into new, larger buildings at Weymouth. The name was then changed to the *Weymouth Free Press*. Another four-page weekly, *L'Acadie Liberale*, was published in 1890 at Meteghan "but like the others advocating claims of a particular Party, its life was short and comparatively uneventful." Internal squabbling at the *Free Press* in Weymouth led to the establishment of two newspapers at Digby c. 1900: *The Sissiboo Echo* and *L'Acadie*. Neither lasted very long, and *L'Évangeline* was moved to Moncton, N.B around 1905. Digby resident John T. McBride established a small daily publication in 1894, *The Telegraph*, which lasted about ten years. McBride followed up with *The Digby County Record* in 1908, printing it first in Weymouth, then at Annapolis, but this weekly survived only two years. The village of Bear River printed its own newspaper, the *Bear River Telephone* c. 1897-1907, which eventually merged with the *Weekly Monitor* in Bridgetown to form *The Monitor & Annapolis Sentinel*. In 1931 the *Weymouth Gazette* made a comeback but lasted only three years, due to lack of advertising.

DIGBY POOR HOUSE 1891-1963

With the County Incorporation Act of 1879, most counties became responsible for building a poor house—although an earlier practice of boarding out paupers, sometimes to the lowest bidder at public auction, continued in some parts of the province. "Poor houses"—a term often used interchangeably with alms houses, county homes, county farms and asylums—"became dumping grounds for all kinds of human misery, including the mentally ill, the severely retarded, unmarried mothers, children and anyone who could not get by in the community or who happened to offend the moral code of the time." Records indicate that Digby County had a poor house prior to 1879, but few details exist. Joseph Thibault, the alms house keeper at that time, was charged with murder in "one of the most horrible and sensational" cases ever tried in Nova Scotia. Subsequently found guilty of brutally killing a female "inmate," Thibault's hanging at Digby on February 8, 1881 was witnessed by a frenzied crowd of eight hundred who "in their eagerness to see the spectacle, tore down a twenty-foot fence that obstructed their view of the gallows." In 1890 the Digby Municipal Council paid a thousand dollars for Robert Marshall's farm at nearby Marshalltown as the site for a new poor house. Despite the fact that the general public "was strongly opposed in every legitimate manner throughout its course" this alms house was built in 1891 and opened for business a year later. In 1897, Clare Municipality in the County of Digby opened its own poor house at Meteghan, which by all accounts was one of the better-run institutions in the province. Always at the mercy of the keeper, stories of abuse and neglect are legion from those unfortunates who experienced life at the county poor houses. However, one keeper's name "became a synonym in Digby for Christian kindness." During the throes of the Great Depression keeper Guy Thomas is said to have "fed half of Digby County from the Poor Farm." Closed in 1963, the last vestiges of the Marshalltown Poor House vanished in 1995 with an arson's match.

Digby has had three hospitals, the second of which, pictured here, opened on April 28, 1931. It replaced the town's first hospital, opened in April 1925 in rented hotel space on the corner of Warwick and West Streets. The cost of the new 32-bed hospital was $45,000; the money raised through contributions, bazaars and the diligent

work of the Ladies Hospital Aid Society and Digby's four doctors: DuVernet, Read, Roberts, and Dickie. An X-ray machine was installed in March, 1935.

Digby's earliest doctors were Christian Tobias, Peter Huggeford, John Skinner, Fleming Pinckston, and Joseph Marvin. William Young and William Schirmer were listed as medical practitioners in Sept. 1789. Later doctors were J. E. Jones (1880), Fred S. Kinsman (1891), Edward Duvernet (1893), and a Dr. Morse.

A man by the name of Sachet and his only child succumbed to the dreaded smallpox disease shortly after arriving in 1783, and are reputed to be the first Loyalist settlers buried in Digby. Smallpox claimed many lives, as did cancer and work-related accidents associated with tree fellings and drownings. A check of burial registers lists an interesting array of maladies afflicting Digby residents: mortification, consumption, quick consumption, hemorrhage, grief, dropsy, fistula, pleurisy, nervous fever, asthma, abscess, ulcers, apoplexy, nasal palsy, convulsion fits, quinsy, fever sores, yellow fever, cholera, nervous disorder, and putrid fever. Despite the many afflictions faced in these early Digby days, those living past the age of an octogenarian were common, one of the oldest being Susannah Smith, buried at Digby on September 24, 1824, aged 110 years.

A 1918 World War I photo taken in Belgium of 20-year old Digby native Guy Victor Turnbull. William Turnbull, Guy Victor's grandfather, emigrated with his family in 1786 from Scotland because of wide-spread famine and became the first to settle at Bay View, a once-prosperous community four miles north of Digby

town. In 1893, William's son George Dykeman Turnbull (1864-1906), a doctor, married Digby school teacher Jessie Stuart Titus (1869-1942). They had three sons: John Fulton, who went on to become a Forestry Engineer in Ontario; George Archer, killed in 1916 during fighting in France; and Guy Victor, who practiced dentistry at Digby until the age of seventy-three. George Turnbull, a medical graduate of Dalhousie University in Halifax, moved his family to Yarmouth in 1896 where he practiced medicine for ten years before his death in 1906 from what a family source claims was radiation-induced illness associated with the pioneer useage of the X-ray machine. Jessie Turnbull then returned to Digby with her sons and lived out her days in a house on Queen Street. Guy Victor Turnbull served in both world wars, rising to the rank of Lieutenant Colonel, and was Canadian Legion Digby Branch's first president. A respected community leader, he served two terms on Town Council, seven years on Digby School Board, was president of Digby Home & School, Treasurer of the Western Nova Scotia Yacht Club, and initiated the Cub movement in Digby, leading the 1st Cub Pack for 11 years. Dr. Turnbull was also Warden of Trinity Church and on vestry for 30 years. An avid outdoorsman in his leisure time, Guy Victor Turnbull passed away in 1986 at the age of 88 years.

In January 1886, a *Digby Courier* editorial urged the town to purchase a fire engine as insurance companies had recently raised fire rates. In November of that year, a meeting was held to organize a fire department. Thirty citizens volunteered as firemen, with elected officers being G.A. Viets, Captain; John Daley, Foreman; Henry Dakin, Assistant Foreman; James M. Keen, 1st Engineer; and E.C. Dodge, 2nd Engineer. Plans were made for ten water tanks, each containing twelve hundred gallons of water, to be strategically placed around town; an electrical bell system was to be installed to connect the homes of each fireman (electricity did not arrive, however, until 1891). In mid-November of 1886, the new steam fire engine arrived at Digby, ordered from Yarmouth's Burril-Johnson Iron Company and accompanied by members of the Yarmouth Fire Company. The fire engine was not used until late 1890; the building burned to the ground, and concerns were raised over an apparent lack of upkeep on the water storage tanks and the non-existence of alarm bells. In September 1900, the new Digby Fire/Town Hall, pictured here, was opened on Sydney Street. Designed by D.F. Young of Digby and built by S.M. Comeau from Meteghan River, the lower floor had space for storing fire apparatus and drying hose, with rooms for the firemen and the water superintendent's office. The Town Clerk's office, Council Chamber, stipendiary magistrate's office, and a meeting room were on the second floor. The attic, while not yet then finished, had a stairway leading to the tower. In 1918 the Digby Fire Department had 25 men, 2 hose houses, 3 hose reels with 1,500 feet of hose, a ladder cart, and a hook and ladder. There were 22 hydrants throughout the town. A fire siren was finally installed in April 1929, and in the summer of 1935 Fire Chief Harry Hersey organized the Digby Jr. Fire Department. The brigade was comprised of 15 members ranging from 10-15 years of age, and claimed to be the first of its kind in the province.

**DIGBY
POWER
PLANT,
c. 1899**

Digby town first turned on to electricty in 1891 when Carman O'Dell from
Annapolis Royal and Digby's H.A.P. Smith organized the Digby Electric Light
Company to service commercial and domestic customers. Amherst's Canada
Electric Company and A. Robb & Sons provided equipment and installation.
Charges were based on rates rather than metres; the following annual charges
applied to the incandescent light of 16-candle-power lamps:

Drawing room, used only as such $6.00, remainder $3.00
Upper Hall $5.00, remainder $3.00
Bedrooms not used as sitting rooms $3.00
Lower Halls $5.00, remainder $3.00
Parlours, sitting rooms and general living rooms $8.00, remaining $3.00
Kitchen and Dining rooms $6.00, remaining $3.00
Bathrooms, Attics, Closets, Cellars, etc. $2.00
Stores, Offices and all commercial lights 3 cents per night

According to R. Baden Powell's account in *Second Scrap Book*, Digby Town &
Municipality, these rates carried certain conditions:

"The subscriber agreed to keep all lights, not actually required, turned off. All lights
were to be put out as soon as a shop or other commercial establishment closed for
the night. Double rates (6 cents per night) were charged for commercial lights
burning after 10 P.M. unless in actual use. The Company ran the service wires to the
house, free of charge. All work done in the house and all lamps, fixtures and
fittings were paid for and owned by the subscriber."

One of the many buildings consumed in the Fire of 1899 was the Turnbull Block post office. Accounts of the time state that not a single piece of mail was lost in the raging inferno, thanks to the heroic efforts of Fred and Bernard McBride and John Robinson. A new brick post office, pictured here, was built on Water Street in 1903, its clock tower having an $1,800 illuminated dial.

Digby's first postmaster was Andrew Snodgrass who established a post office

c. 1784 in the front room of his home on the west side of Water Street just north of the Baptist Church. "One of the first privileges enjoyed by the shire town," according to county historian Isaiah Wilson, "was mail communication weekly with Halifax by way of Annapolis. A 'courier' left the Capital each Monday at 2 o'clock in the afternoon for the west and on following Wednesday reached Kentville. Here the courier who left Digby at [the] same time, James Baxter, arrived. Mails were exchanged; and each returned to his home conveying safely whatever was received. Riding primarily on horseback they carried the mails in saddle bags." Wilson also tells us that mail travelling between Digby and Yarmouth prior to 1810 was "entrusted to any Acadian who happened to be travelling from either point to the other. This exemplifies their unflinching honesty, even with a foreign power." An Order of Council was in fact issued on October 25, 1775 making it mandatory that all dispatches be conveyed by French Acadians who were to be paid five shillings per diem for their services.

After 1810, with the opening of a post road between Digby and Yarmouth, Jesse Wyman from Yarmouth was the first courier hired for weekly service between the towns, riding on horseback with the mail safely tucked away in his coat pocket or a saddle bag from which he made door to door deliveries enroute. Mail also travelled weekly via sailing packets between Digby and Saint John, N.B. from the earliest arrival of Loyalist settlers.

BANK OF NOVA SCOTIA 1899-1970

Enos Collins established the forerunner of the Bank of Nova Scotia in 1825 when he opened the province's first private banking business from his warehouse in Halifax. The Bank of Nova Scotia building here was erected on Digby's Water Street in 1899 from plans designed by architect William Critchlow Harris (1854-1913) whose brother Robert Harris was Prince Edward Island's noted portrait painter. Robert C. Tuck's *Gothic Dreams: Life and Times of a Canadian Architect*

describes W.C. Harris as "a talented and original High Victorian architect, trained entirely in Canada" who built churches, banks, office buildings, courthouses, libraries, and other civic and private structures in Nova Scotia. In addition to the Bank of Nova Scotia, Harris also drew plans for the main building at College Sainte-Anne at Church Point, an addition to the Evangeline Hotel in Digby, and a new Turnbull building on Water Street to replace one destroyed in the 1899 fire. Of the four Harris designs, only the College Sainte-Anne structure remains. The Bank of Nova Scotia, "was constructed of rock-faced stone with multicoloured brick surrounds at the windows and doorways and what appears to be from its photograph a slate roof," decribes Tuck. "It was very solidly built, and a building of some architectural distinction. In 1970 it was torn down by the Bank of Nova Scotia and replaced by a brick and glass box of bland appearance. The old building would have made an admirable town hall for the town of Digby, but the bank apparently thought only of its need for increased floor space, and so it was demolished in an act that impoverished Digby and diminished the Bank of Nova Scotia."

ROYAL BANK EMPLOYEES

The Royal Bank of Canada developed from a financial partnership started in 1864 at Halifax known as the Bank of the Seven Merchants. This photo of three young bank employees was taken inside what is thought to be the Royal Bank of Canada's Digby branch office. A 1910 advertisement in the *Digby Courier* claimed that Royal Bank of Canada assets totalled $95 million and encouraged deposits: "The Savings Department of this Bank provides a safe place for your savings to accumulate, and grow with the Interest which is added half-yearly. $1.00 or upward is enough for the first deposit. Money may be withdrawn whenever required. No man remains poor who saves every week, or month, or year, a certain amount, no matter how small. Few ever get rich without doing so."

Photographer Paul Yates was born in 1863 at Philadelphia, Pennsylvania. After working in advertising and commercial photography for some years in the United States, Yates came to Annapolis Royal c. 1906 and opened a commercial photography studio. A couple of years later he moved his family to Digby and opened "The Little Art Gallery" on Water Street. Yates continued to split his time between both businesses until the Annapolis studio burned in March 1921. When his wife Dorothy died, he married Jeanette W. VanTassell, who was employed in the Digby

studio. Although Yates was often commissioned to take individual and family portraits, as well as business photographs (especially for hotel advertising), his specialty was scenic photography. Many scenes were turned into postcards, while others toured North America for showings. Yates was often accompanied on his photographic sojourns by renowned photographer W.A. MacAskill. Jeanette Yates assumed an active role in the business, eventually taking all studio portraits and being responsible for much of the developing and printing. Following her husband's death in 1946, Jeanette continued to operate the Digby studio until 1968, mostly selling reprints of her husband's earlier work; she passed away in 1970. Sadly, only a few hundred of Paul Yates's thousands of negatives survive today, most being in the Public Archives of Nova Scotia in Halifax, taken between 1910 and 1935. Sometime around 1960, Jeanette Yates notified the landlord of her rented studio building that the ceiling there was noticeably sagging. Upon inspection it was discovered the cause was from the sheer weight of the numbers of glass negatives stored in the attic. Ordered to remove the hazard at once, Yates saved only a few boxes of negatives thought useful for postcards, then hired two boys with snow shovels to throw the remainder of Digby's history out the window and onto the rocky shores of the Annapolis Basin below.

POINT PRIM LIGHTHOUSE

POINT PRIM LIGHTHOUSE

Point Prim Lighthouse was built in 1817 on the west side of the Digby Gut entrance to the Annapolis Basin. Known then as the "Fundy Light," its first keeper was Richard Bragg from England, who held the post for 56 years until he was replaced in 1873 by Sheppard J. Frost. Captain William Ensley Ellis assumed light-keeper duties in 1876, at a yearly salary of eight hundred dollars. In July 1887, he discovered the Ellis Comet, named in his honour years later by the world's leading astronomers. His appointment began a family tradition that would last 85 years. Captain Ellis operated the light from 1876 until his death in 1912, when Leander Montgomery Ellis, eldest son of 15 children, took his father's place. Leander Ellis worked the light for 22 years until his retirement in 1934, when duties were passed to his son-in-law Frank Wilson, who carried on for another 27 years. The line of Ellis lightkeepers ended in 1963 with Frank Wilson's death, at which time Carman Frankland transfered to Point Prim from Ganet Rock light.

A dull, smoky, whale-oil lamp for the signal light and a swivel gun for fog warnings were used at Point Prim until 1871; kerosene lighting and a steam whistle were then installed. This system was replaced in 1911 by the kerosene vapour lamp and an oil-fired, compressed-air fog horn. It was the women's daily responsibility to clean and refill the 12 kerosene lamps in the lighthouse tower. Next came the electrically-powered light and diesel engine, which was followed by a fully-automated, unmanned beacon. The original Point Prim lighthouse burned to the ground on March 16, 1873, but was immediately replaced by the one pictured here, which stood until it was demolished in 1964 in favor of a modern concrete structure.

BAY VIEW LIFE SAVING STATION

Nestled at the water's edge, near the present-day Digby-Saint John Ferry Terminal, sits the Bay View Life Saving Station. Now keeping only a "ghostly vigilance over

the area it once served so faithfully," the station was established c. 1911 to render assistance to vessels in distress on the Annapolis Basin and Fundy coastal waters. A feature of this photo is the marine railway leading up to the building, where the lifeboat could be hauled out and under cover for repairs or storage. In its early years, the station came under the jurisdiction of the Naval Service and received supplies from the Halifax Dockyard. Following World War I, responsibility shifted to the Department of Marine and Fisheries, then to the Department of Transport Marine Services (Canadian Coast Guard) in the early 1930s. Its days as an operational facility came to an end at noon on Monday, March 9, 1970, in favour of a station in Westport on Brier Island.

LIFEBOAT *DARING*

The original lifeboat operated from the Bay View station until it was replaced with a smaller but better-equipped model in 1951, after 40 years of service. The first boat, aptly named *Daring*, was built of mahogany, its hull diagonally planked, finished with oak rails and copper fastened. Thirty-six feet in length, self-bailing

and self-uprighting, she had a variety of power sources: oars, removable mast and sails, and a German six-cylinder gasoline motor. The *Daring* was built in Bayonne, New Jersey, arriving in Saint John, N.B. on a flat-bed railway car and turned over to the Bayview crew. During her years of service, the indomitable little vessel extracted many a 'daring' rescue on the stormy Bay of Fundy waters. During World War I, she ferried Digby doctors to foreign ships under quarantine, which were occasionally required to anchor in the Annapolis Basin.

LIFESAVING CREW, C. 1920

Pictured here are the original crew members who manned the Bay View Life Saving Station: (L-R) Wallace Abbott, Orbin Condon, Ed Bremner, Albert (Bub) Hersey, Fred Adams, Jim Ellis, Samuel Edgar Wilson. Missing from the photo is John Hayden. In the 59-year history of the station, only six coxwains were in charge of the lifeboat. Listed in order of earliest command was John W. Hayden, Orbin Condon, Wm. Snow, Harry Raymond, Hilyard Barns, and Harry Adams. In the late 1920s, the lifesaving station was shut down for a while, except for a couple of caretakers who maintained the premises until the station re-opened in 1927.

In the beginning the crew consisted of eight men, but in the 1930s its complement was reduced to seven, with shifts covering two-hour "around the clock" watches. The lifesaving crew remained at seven (each man working six days with two off) until 1969, when numbers were cut to six (making two, three-man teams). When the station closed in 1970, Eugene Burns, who joined in 1935, held the distinction of serving the longest term of any man to have worked aboard the lifesaving boat at Bay View Station.

SCHOONER *AGNES G. DONAHOE*, POINT PRIM 1913

Today, a monument bearing 149 names sits in front of the Digby post office. Topped by a hand-operated bell—once used at North Point, Brier Island to warn mariners of shoals—the inscription reads "In Proud Memory of All the Seafaring Sons of Annapolis Basin, Digby Neck and Islands Area Who Were Lost At Sea During the Period of 1867-1967." Point Prim was the scene of many wrecks over the years, one being the schooner *Agnes G. Donahoe,* which foundered in 1913, without loss of life, while laden with a cargo of bricks. Three miles west of Point Prim, the settlement of Broad Cove was renamed "Culloden" in recognition of a British vessel by that name which was driven ashore there in 1859 during an autumn gale. Fundy winter storms were the worst, a northeaster one time driving the Ellis family from their lighthouse home when waves washed through an upstairs bedroom window and flooded the kitchen below. It was during a similar tempest in December 1883 that the government steamship *Princess Louise* met her end at Christopher's Bluff, only a mile and a quarter west of Point Prim. The S.S. *Newfield* was towing the vessel from Canning when the line parted, leaving the vulnerable *Princess Louise* to be driven onto the rocks. Eight of ten crew members were drowned (keeper Leander Ellis saved the others), prompting the Dominion Government to erect a monument in their memory. Ironically the S.S. *Newfield* was wrecked in later years near the same site. Point Prim was itself named in reference to a marine disaster. Long known as Roger's Point after this British Major and his Rangers massacred Mi'kmaq there in the 1750s, the name was changed to "Prim Point" or "Point Prim" in the 1800s to commemorate a Black man by the name of Prim—the sole survivor of a wreck—whose shipmates were buried on the point.

Chapter 4

Special Events

SIR WILFRED LAURIER VISITS DIGBY

"Digby was honoured with other Towns of the Province by occasional visits of Governors and other public dignitaries." In 1794, Edward, Duke of Kent, "was given a Banquet and witnessed other unmistakeable demonstrations of respect and attachment during his brief sojourn." Sir James Kempt, King's representative, toured Digby c. 1820, as did Lord and Lady Falkland in 1844. The Prince of Wales—later King George V—is said to have had his shoes shined by Hardy Bent during a brief stop at Digby. The Marquis of Lorne, Governor General of Canada, and companion Princess Louise Caroline Alberta, sixth child of Queen Victoria, were entertained with a reception in August 1880 at John Daley's Royal Hotel. Governor General and Lady Byng visited Digby in August 1923. Canadian Prime Ministers Sir Wilfred Laurier (seated to left in this photo), Richard Bennett, and McKenzie King all campaigned at Digby on their political travels. Knighted in London at Queen Victoria's 1897 Diamond Jubilee celebrations, Laurier (1841-1919) served the longest unbroken term of any Canadian prime minister—1896-1911.

Digby Regatta, 1872

CHAMPION SCULLER GEORGE BROWN

Digby was the scene of frenzied excitement during the summer of 1872 when noted oarsmen George Brown from Halifax, N.S. and Robert Fulton from Saint John, N.B. squared off in Digby Harbour for a sculling race. With Brown's fans bedecked in blue and Fulton's camp wearing pink, it must have been a colorful occasion. Isaiah Wilson described the event in his county history:

"The affair occurred between seven and eight o'clock, July 12th. The Course was from a point off the Joggins, about three-fourths of a mile to southeast of the town in a straight line, ending at two boats moored about half a mile above Indian Beach, being four miles from commencement of the Course. It was almost parallel with the track of steamers plying between Saint John and Digby. Brown won the laurels by about five boat lengths; the time occupied in rowing the distance was twenty minutes and forty seconds. Fulton appeared unusually nervous; and his strokes though numbering forty to the minute—lacked finish and strength. His friends from Saint John attributed the defeat to an inferior boat; but the consensus averred that Brown was superior personally."

George Brown, who has been described as "one of Nova Scotia's first and greatest racers" returned to Halifax a hero, as cheering crowds lined the railway tracks from Annapolis to the capital city where a torch light parade awaited his arrival.

The Digby Regatta was organized in hopes that "capital should accompany the venture" but the feeling was that similar endeavours in the future would not be feasible, as the broad expanse of the Annapolis Basin lent itself "too often disturbed by winds and currents from the Bay [of Fundy], to make boat racing in its waters profitable or expedient."

CONTROVERSY MARRED THE 1872 DIGBY REGATTA

Three thousand spectators lined the harbour shore to cheer on the participants of the Four-Oared Lapstreak Race, won by the Digby entry over the more highly-touted Ross-Foley crew. "The excitement was intense though tempered with moderate exhibitions by the respectable," wrote Isaiah Wilson. "Unfortunately however, the cheap excursion on steamers from Saint John, N.B., induced a multitude of roughs from abroad to visit the hitherto quiet town. Consequently, though sixty special constables were provided, yet repeated and desperate cases of rowdyism pervaded the transactions....Drunkeness and fighting were frequently observable during the week. Never had Digby witnessed such unseemly and daring conduct by such overpowering and reckless specimans of humanity....The majority of desperadoes having returned in the *Scud* that afternoon, comparative order was restored. The exercise clearly demonstrated that such proceedings invariably attract the most vicious and depraved, who set law and decorum at defiance." In light of these developments some scheduled races were cancelled "to avoid any unpleasant feelings which might ensue." Sportsmanship prevailed in some circles, however, as friends of George Brown raised $250 for Robert Fulton and "the best feeling prevailed between admirers of both the principals in that memorable drama."

FISHERMEN'S REGATTA

Crowds gather at the bandstand on August 19, 1913 to take in the festivities at the Digby Fishermen's Regatta. This was the third year for the gala event that had been organized in 1911 by Mayor Harry Short, O.S. Dunham (editor of the *Digby Courier*) and Captain Howard Anderson (superintendent of Maritime Fish Corporation's Digby plant). Water Street and Montague Row were bedecked with flags, bunting, and banners. Thousands of spectators are said to have taken in the two-day festivities, arriving by train, automobile, boat, buggy, ox cart, and on foot. From Yarmouth to Middleton they came, jamming the waterfront with the hundreds of tourists who made Digby home during the summer months. Events got underway at 7:00 A.M. with a 35-mile, three-hour race from Tiverton to Digby, involving a flotilla of small motorized fishing boats. By the time of their arrival, dory races were in full swing, as were heats featuring gasoline-powered pleasure boats that "competed with one another in speed and noise....Shrieking sirens, clanging bells and raucous foghorns added to the clamour. Even the summer 'rusticators,' Americans mostly, caught the spirit of the thing and yelled, cheered and betted with enthusiastic impartiality." Amid the cacophonous din, Mi'kmaq guides from Bear River demonstrated their paddling expertise in bark canoes, more a show than a race for cash.

Fly Casting at the Fishermen's Regatta

The Baptist church spire, Manhatten Hotel, and Public Pavillion backdrop this
photo of fly-casting competitors at the Fishermen's Regatta. An added attraction for
1913 was the annual Nova Scotia Guides Association Meet held that year at Digby.
More than a hundred guides pitched tents on Battery Point and competed in a
one-day competition of trout and salmon fly casting (for accuracy and distance)
rifle and trap shooting, log chopping, kettle boiling, moose calling, and story
telling. Water sports were another popular feature: log burling, single and double
canoe races, tub races, and novel events such as canoe filling and canoe rescue. At
day's end, a general meeting of guides was held to discuss issues of business and
conservation pertaining to their profession, and to hand out individual and over-all
champion awards. It was reported the Digby meet was "the most successful in the
history of the Guides who proved themselves very good sports with excellent
behavior."

Brittain Cup Races of 1911 & 1912

ALBERT J. LUTZ

Ten years before Lunenburg's *Bluenose* sailed to fame in the International Fishermen's Races out of Halifax and Gloucester, Digby was host in 1911 to a schooner race of smaller scale but of no less historical significance for its time. From its launch in 1908 at Joseph McGill's Shelburne shipyard, the 95-ton, 90-foot long *Albert J. Lutz* (pictured here) was the "Queen of the Digby fleet." An argument could be made that she was the best in the entire Nova Scotia Bank fishing fleet. Her skipper and part-owner, Captain John Apt, hailed from Port Wade on the Annapolis shore of the Basin, and because of this was seen by many in Digby as being "from away," as was any crew that sailed with him. It mattered little that the schooner landed her fish in Digby, that she was registered and partly owned in Digby, and that many who sailed on her had their homes in Digby—they were nonetheless Port Waders. As such, the *Lutz* "was regarded as a serious rival to the honour and supremacy of the port of Digby in those days." Envy and competitive feelings such as these gave rise to the Brittain Cup, reportedly the first of its kind ever awarded for schooner racing in Nova Scotia.

DOROTHY M. SMART

The schooner *Dorothy M. Smart*, named in honour of Maritime Fish Corporation President Colonel Charles A. Smart's daughter, was launched from the McGill Shelburne yards in 1910. Built at a cost of ten thousand dollars from plans drawn by prominent Boston designer T.E. McManus, her role was twofold: increased catch quotas for the owner, Maritime Fish Corporation, and (perhaps more important) to beat the *Albert J. Lutz*. Some say the latter was the sole reason she was built. Equal in length, with only one ton separating them in weight, the two vessels met head to head at the inaugural 1911 Digby Fishermen's Regatta. At stake was the Brittain Cup, a silver trophy donated by Alfred H. Brittain, general manager for Maritime Fish Corporation. All other events at the Fishermen's Regatta paled in comparison, as this was the heavyweight clash that thousands of spectators thronged to Digby to witness. Amid much hoopala, the *Dorothy M. Smart*, with Captain Harry Ross at the helm, trimmed the *Albert J. Lutz*, "sea-worn" from a summer's fishing and under-crewed to boot, by a scant 95 seconds over the 12 mile course around Goat Island. Captain John Apt is acknowledged to have sailed the better race, bringing the *Lutz* from far back to finish "like smoke—a creaming froth at her forefoot, her sails set as though in marble." It mattered little in the end as the *Dorothy M. Smart* was crowned undisputed champion of the fishing fleet, at least for the time being. In the prophetic words of Captain Harry Ross, "Next time may be a different story."

Frederick William Wallace described Captain Harry Ross in *Roving Fisherman* as "boyish in his general appearance, in his quiet manner of speech" but having the reputation as a "resourceful fisherman, a good 'fish killer,' and a resolute character, a 'driver,' fearless and daring." Harry Ross first captained a Digby fishing schooner at

21 years of age and was only 24 at the time of the first Brittain Cup Race. In 1911, while captain of the *Dorothy M. Smart*, Ross landed 1,676,915 pounds of fish in the span of 12 months. A record for the time, it earned Captain Ross the prestigious title of "high line" skipper for the fishing fleet. Over the years his reputation as a high-liner grew, as he captained a number of vessels including the *Effie M. Morrissey* and the Boston-based fresh fishing schooner *Morning Star*. During Prohibition, Captain Ross "was one of the most successful skippers in the "rum-running fleet" and pulled off a number of daring excursions through the Volstead Blockade." Captain Harry Ross died in November 1953 at his home in Dorchester, Mass. The *Dorothy M. Smart*, after a varied 20-year career of being a fisherman, rum-runner, and coaster was wrecked in 1930 near Cape Negro, Shelburne County.

It has been said of Captain John Apt that "what he didn't know about handling vessels wasn't worth knowing." A legendary figure throughout the fishing fraternity "he was a natural-born sailorman who combined the business of fishing with the thrill to be had from getting the best out of the vessel he sailed, in any weather, any time and any place."

Defeat did not sit well with him and, in a rematch for the Brittain Cup in 1912 at the Digby Fishermen's Regatta, Apt had the *Lutz* in fighting trim and fully crewed. The importance of the second race was evidenced by the attendence of Canada's Royal Governor General, the Duke and Duchess of Connaught, their daughter the Princess Patricia, as well as yachtsmen from New York and the Royal Kennebeccasis Yacht Club in Saint John, N.B. The second race was no contest. John Apt was a formidable opponent to any who dared challenge his championship mantle, "for every vessel that he met and was prepared to hoist canvas against him, his beloved *Lutz* left them astern." And leave the *Dorothy M. Smart* astern they did on this occasion, by a full 13 minutes at the finish. The Brittain Cup was Apt's for all time, never contested again. Today it resides on display at the Maritime Museum of the Atlantic in Halifax.

In October 1915, while skippering the *Albert J. Lutz* off Cape Sable, Captain Apt, 47, was stricken by a sudden attack of appendicitis. Transferred to a coasting steamer and taken to Saint John hospital, he died on the operating table. In 1919, his beloved *Lutz* met her end. After surviving World War I as a German U-boat hunting Q-ship, she was sold to Newfoundland fishing interests and, while enroute to her new owners, capsized off Cape Broyle.

Digby at War, 1914-1918

FENIAN RAID VETERANS

On September 9, 1914, the Digby veterans who defended Canada a half century earlier against the Fenian raiders gathered for this Paul Yates photo on the steps of the Digby court house.

Based in the United States in the mid-1800s, the Fenians were an Irish nationalist society who promoted (sometimes violent) anti-British activity. They have been described as "one of the strangest organizations that ever affected Canada's history." At the close of the American Civil War the extreme element in their midst "had the wild idea of conquering Canada and making it a base to conquer England." The U.S. government showed no interest in curbing their militaristic activities, and its newspapers only fueled the fires by spreading anti-British propaganda and threats of annexation.

In the spring of 1866, armed bands of Fenians gathered at the border from Detroit to New Brunswick and ten thousand Canadian men were subsequently rallied to repel the invaders. In May some six hundred Fenians attacked across the Niagara River from Buffalo, and during the ensuing skirmish at Ridgeway, nine of its members were killed. The Fenians remained a thorn in Canada's side until the early 1870s but never a real threat. In his book Building the Canadian Nation, George Brown writes that "Canadians were aroused by the invasion of Canadian soil....It is a curious fact in Canadian history that the Fenians unintentionally did a great service to the cause of Confederation."

112TH BATTALION, 1916

Soldiers of the 112th Battalion form up in front of the Waverly Hotel at the corner of Birch and Prince William Streets. One hundred and thirteen recruits from the 112th trained at Digby in 1916. At the same time, the 29th Battalion dispersed a number of its men throughout the county for training—42 at Digby, 43 in Weymouth, 62 in Bear River, and 38 at Tiverton. The long, low building with many windows in the background of this photo was called the Iron Duke and served as a drill shed during World War I. It was named, some say, for the Duke of Wellington (1769-1852), a British general and statesman who defeated Napoleon at Waterloo in 1815 and served as Britain's prime minister from 1828-1830. The Iron Duke was built as a fish processing plant between 1890 and 1910, and other sources attribute the name to the miles of iron pipe then used in its mechanical fish-drying equipment. Still standing today, an interesting feature is the open passageway through the building's centre, which gave fishermen access to and from the harbour front wharves and beach.

237TH AMERICAN LEGION ENCAMPMENT AT THE RACQUETTE

When militia units encamped on Green Point at the Racquette, the rank and file tented while officers billeted at the Pines Hotel, as featured in this 1916 Paul Yates photo. An interesting anecdote connects Green Point with the Admiral Robert Digby of 119 years earlier. In the autumn of 1797, while patrolling the Bay of Fundy in search of privateers, Admiral Digby anchored his warship *Wye* at the Racquette so as "to visit the town and survey its surroundings." A sudden freeze trapped his vessel in ice, leaving the Admiral stranded until spring break-up, but at the same time ensuring Digby town "thoroughly safe...from remorseless foreign pirates." Admiral Digby no doubt wintered in relative warmth and comfort at a house he had built c. 1790 at 3 Maiden Lane. History tells us, however, that his "brave associates" were left to clear Green Point of timber for winter fuel and a Lewis Cossett, who owned a farm several miles away near the mouth of the Bear River, "supplied the *Wye* whatever was required during her stay."

ARRIVAL OF 4TH PIONEERS IN DIGBY, 1917

TOP RIGHT

The third year of the Great War was a busy one for Digby, militia units coming and going aboard the Saint John ferry or troop trains to Halifax. When the 237th American Legion moved out, the 4th Pioneers arrived, its 943 men and officers shown here marching along Racquette Road to the Green Point encampment. In September, the Pioneers were replaced by the 209th Battalion—consisting of 920 men recruited from Swift Current, Saskatchewan. They stayed until October preparations for shipment overseas.

DIGBY ARMY CADETS

BOTTOM
RIGHT

Strong character, morals, and discipline based on God, country, King and family were the bulwark of societal values instilled by youth military training. Identified in this group shot of army cadets, taken c. 1914 on the Digby Court House steps are (L-R) *Front Row*: John Wightman, Harry Snow, Roy Warner, James Dillon, Lorne Hayden, Cedric Robertson, G. Victor Turnbull (Company Commander). *2nd Row*: Benny Webber, Hubert Warne, Louis Morse, Lorne Hutchinson, Arthur Caity, Fred Muise, George MacKay, Will Perry. *3rd Row*: Mr. Hogg, Principal, Perry Cousins, Eric Morse, Digby Winchester, Kingsley Collins, Arthur Lochley, ? Warrington, George Morine. 4th. Row: Harris Dillon, Chester Budd, Boyd German, ? VanTassel, Donald McInnis, Boyd Milberry, Oakley Turnbull, Donald Winchester.

ARRIVAL OF 4TH PIONEERS (ABOVE) AND DIGBY ARMY CADETS (BELOW)

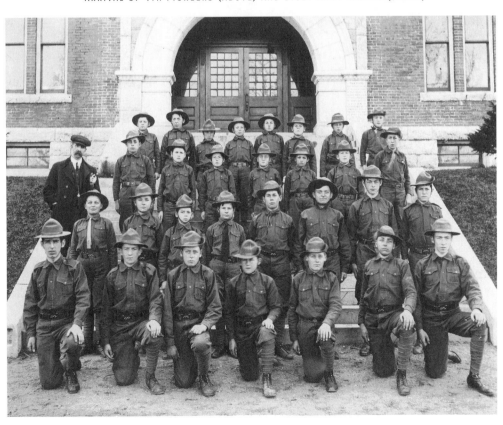

JUVENILE RED CROSS ENTERTAINMENT

On the home front, everyone had a part to play in defeating the Kaiser, even these entertaining Digby youngsters, part of the Juvenile Red Cross on August 15, 1918. Virtually every community in Digby County organized a Red Cross Unit to knit socks and sweaters and to raise money for the Patriotic Relief Fund. At the behest of the federal government, boys too young to fight at Vimy and Passchendaele left school and, as "Soldiers of the Soil," marched off to the fields to meet increased demands for farm produce. It was the best and worst of times. Wages for labour work rose from 10 to 30 cents an hour, but food prices sky-rocketed because of a scaracity that was due, in large measure, to paranoid hoarding of emergency household staples. Women won the right to vote, but it was limited to those who had a son or husband in the forces or stationed at the Front. War bonds were peddled door to door, and conscription became a hot political issue. Daylight Saving Time was introduced as a war measure in 1917 to allow more time for increased farm production. The federal government assumed responsibility from provincial authorities to collect income tax as a 'temporary measure' to fill the war chests. The price of mailing a letter increased 50% to three cents, the extra cent levied as a war tax. In 1918, doctors watched helplessly as the Spanish Flu made its appearance, a plague responsible for killing more than all the battlefields of World War I.

DIGBY WAR MONUMENT, WATER STREET

When word of the German Kaiser's abdication reached the Western Union Telegraph office at Digby on Saturday November 9, 1918, pandemonium broke loose in the streets. Guns blasted, with horns and bells creating an ear-splitting din. It was said the electric light plant blew off so much steam sounding the fire whistle that the plant had to shut down until steam could be built up to generate electricity. Sunday was a day of thanksgiving services in all the town and surrounding churches. When the Armistice was officially announced in Digby on Monday November 11 at 7:40 A.M., council declared a public holiday for 11:30 A.M. The day was taken up with joyous celebration, including a morning thanksgiving service at the Court House, afternoon parade along Water Street, and a concluding bonfire on the hill above town, which lit up the evening sky for miles around. Festivities continued into Tuesday with the announcement of a federal holiday. By Wednesday the gaity had died down, and Digby town and county began the transition to postwar life. On August 18, 1920, Rossway dedicated the first soldiers' memorial to war dead. Similar monuments were erected during the 1920s-30s at Digby, Weymouth, Barton, Smith's Cove, Bear River, Freeport, and Little River. The names of 17 killed in World War I and 19 in World War II appear on the Digby cenotaph.

W.W. II British Merchant Ship *Samzona* off Digby

During World War II, merchant ships were the lifeline of the world as they ferried all manner of supplies, weapons, and troops overseas in support of the Allied war effort. Sailing empty most times from Britain to North American ports, merchant ships loaded up with ballast for added draught needed to brave the treacherous North Atlantic crossing. Not yet designed with double bottoms for water ballast, rubble from bombed-out buildings in British cities was often used. When reaching our eastern seaboard this solid ballast would be dumped in deep water before entering ports like Saint John and Halifax to load up. A favourite drop site for Saint John-bound vessels—like the British merchantman *Samzona* pictured here—was an area off Port Wade on the east shore of Annapolis Basin known as the "Ballast Grounds." It has been said that "much of London and Coventry lies at the bottom of the Annapolis Basin." The war years especially were a busy time for Digby's harbour pilots, whose daunting task it was to board vessels in the Bay of Fundy, most times while under power and often in extreme weather conditions, and guide them safely through Digby Gut to anchorage. Two of the best were said to be John Casey from Victoria Beach and Digby's Harry Raymond, both experienced fishermen and sailors with thorough knowledge of Fundy's treacherous tides and ledges.

Digby was a busy place during the war. Britain was in need of great numbers of pit props for its mines. In 1940 and 1941, more than 123,000 cords of softwood were shipped for this purpose from Nova Scotia, Digby being one of several sites chosen along the coast for a pit prop yard. In 1943, H.M.C.S. *Cornwallis* was built ten miles away in Annapolis County. Encompassing 615 acres, it was the largest establishment of its kind at the time in the British Commonwealth. Eleven thousand naval officers, men, and WRENS went through Cornwallis during World War II, and Digby served as a staging area for training vessels attached to the base.

Oddfellows Hall c. 1911

The Oddfellows Hall on Water Street, with its distinctive peaked tower, was more commonly known as the Bijou Theatre. "For some years Digby had the unfortunate distinction of not possessing a proper public hall," announced the *Digby Courier* in a special 1897 summer edition:

> Concert companies and lecturers frequently passed us by for lack of place whereon to stand. This was certainly a disadvantage and one that plainly must be overcome before Digby could take rank among the up-to-date towns. The Oddfellows came to the rescue and last year [1896] erected the fine two-storey building that is now one of our prides. The lower floor is the public hall. It has a seating capacity of nearly five hundred and is the finest hall of its kind west of Halifax. The scenery, which is exceptionally fine, was made especially in Chicago. The stage is a model one, with electric footlights, and fronted by an orchestra pit. The appointments throughout are of the best and the Oddfellows and Digby are to be congratulated upon the possession of such a fine structure.

Located in the Oddfellow's Hall, the Bijou Dream Theatre replaced the Wonderland, Digby's first moving picture house (opened in 1909). In March 1916, Frederick William Wallace sailed on a two-week voyage aboard Captain Ansel Snow's vessel the *Dorothy G. Snow* to shoot three thousand feet of film documenting the winter hazards of Banks fishing. Costing five hundred dollars to produce, *Seamen Courageous* played to packed houses at the Bijou and, in 1922, to a private audience of movie producers and cameramen at Loew's State Theatre in New York City.

The popularity of the circus is evident in this photo of Water Street lined with spectators for the traditional parade of performers and animals. Digby was a regular stop during the heyday of touring circus companies. In the late 1880s and early 1890s, the Don Driscoll Circus and Don Rice Circus came to town using horse-

drawn wagons. By the late 1890s, Stone & Rowe Circus arrived via the Dominion Atlantic Railway. The John Robinson Circus came in 1919 loaded onto 28 railway cars. Others followed on a nearly yearly basis including Sells Floto Circus (1921), Hagan & Wallace Circus (1922), Sparks Circus (1924,'26) and Bailey Brothers Circus (1928)—the first to use trucks.

Chapter 5

Sports & Leisure

Tennis anyone?

Digby Tennis Club enroute to play a match in Bear River, 1892. Diary entries of school teacher Jessie Titus indicate that Digby did not always fare well in matches against their Bear River opponents.

Friday, May 22, 1892: *"Went to Bear River and got beaten at tennis. Had a very nice time."*

Friday, August 19, 1892: *"Went over to the tennis courts in P.M. Bear River won the match."*

Tennis was a popular late Victorian era sport and a number of Digby hotels and boarding houses advertised private courts for the enjoyment of their summer guests. If this Lewis Rice photo, taken for the Canadian Pacific Railway, wasn't staged for the camera, then the ten-mile coach trip between towns would have been torturously uncomfortable for the passengers featured here.

Hotel "Manhattan," Digby, N.S.

HOTEL "MANHATTAN" c. 1905

The Manhattan Hotel on Montague Row operated from 1900-1913, also managing an annex for additional guests—the Salvia House. When listing the first business proprietors among Digby's Loyalist settlers, historian Isaiah Wilson writes that "James Reid opened a commodious Hotel on southern corner of Water and Mount Streets. Another was founded by Robert Ray on Cruickshank Corner." The number of hotels and boarding houses increased significantly by the late 1800s, with improved steamship service and the arrival of the railway. Some changed names and management often, a case in point being a 30-bedroom inn operated at various times—prior to being demolished in 1961—as the Winchester Hotel, Royal Hotel, Eaton Hotel, and the Travellers Inn. Before radiators were installed in rooms, guests staying here were warmed by heated bricks wrapped in newspapers, or jugs filled with hot water (called 'piggies'). Some other Digby establishments c. 1898 were Myrtle House, Short's Hotel, Evangeline House, Lour Lodge, Parker House, Victoria, Waverly House, Burnham House, Clifford House, Harmony Lodge, Trefry House, and Clinton House.

Lour Lodge, Digby, N. S.

LOUR LODGE

Digby was a mecca for tourists in the early 1900s. Its population doubled to nearly four thousand during summer months from the influx of predominately American vacationers to the town and surrounding countryside. It was estimated for 1903 that tourists spent one hundred thousand dollars in Digby. In 1909, for the month of August alone, the daily average expenditure was three thousand and "nearly all the new buildings erected in the town during the year were either summer cottages owned by the visiters themselves or by natives and leased to tourists." Those who came were from the wealthy class and competition for their business was keen. It has been said that bell boys from various hotels would converge at the DAR station or Steamboat Wharf to await arrivals, the first to reach a prospective looking customer getting the business. Lodging with three meals could be had for as little as $1.50-$2.00 per day, with special rates from $8.00-$10.00 by the week.

Lour Lodge in south end Digby could accomodate 150 guests at the main hotel, annex or eight waterfront cottages which were actually small houses. In 1911, rates for June and September were set at $2-$5 per day or $10 per week, increasing to $12 and up for the months of July and August. Table board was $9 per week. There were three tennis courts and "ample lawns for croquet, one ground laid out expressly for expert players." Occasionally during the summer, a baseball team from Lour Lodge, comprised of tourists and three staff, would play a team of seniors in games that "were hotly contested and exciting at times."

By 1918 Digby had 20 hotels and summer boarding houses, which "are thronged each season with an increasing number of visitors who come to gain the health and strength among its ozone laden forests and enjoy its cool climate and matchless scenery of vale and hillside glen looking out upon its wave-washed harbored shores across the Basin to the Bay of Fundy beyond, which for picturesque beauty has no superior on the Continent." Many were enticed through tour booklets and brochures distributed by the steamship and railway companies that touted Digby

and Digby County as the "Summer Play Place of Nova Scotia." Others came because of promotional efforts by individual operators such as Captain and Mrs. A.T. Spurr who owned Myrtle House. The *Digby Courier* of Dec. 7, 1928 ran the following announcement: "Captain and Mrs. A.T. Spurr of the Myrtle House leave on Tuesday on their annual trip to the United States where they will visit all the important tourist centres along the Atlantic seaboard. They will return early in the Spring to make ready for the opening of the Myrtle House next season." An April 1929 article announced their arrival home, reporting that "ten thousand Myrtle House booklets will be read by prospective visitors to Digby before the end of this present month." It was claimed that this equalled the total number of brochures planned for distribution that year by the newly-formed Land of Evangeline Tourist Association in promoting the entire Annapolis Valley. By the summer of 1935, cruise ships were stopping at Digby, the *Acadia* arriving July 4 from New York via Yarmouth and, a day later, the *Saint John*, which continued making weekly runs from Boston via Saint John throughout the season.

PINES HOTEL

Featured in the following two postcards is the old Pines Hotel, perhaps the grandest of Digby's tourist establishments. Built on a 250-foot elevation at the Racquette, the 3-storey, 60-bedroom hotel gave a magnificent panoramic view of Digby and Annapolis Basin from its four thousand-square-foot veranda. Marguerite Woodworth in her book *History of the Dominion Atlantic Railway* credits Henry Churchill with building "a little hotel" in 1892 and naming it the "Pines"—not after the tree, as there were none around, but because "it had a pleasing sound and

The Pines Hotel, Digby, Nova Scotia.

would attract tourists." In 1903 an H.B. Churchill was reported in the *Digby Courier* to have put up a building at the Pines costing $28,000. Advertised as "a gem of modern architecture and convenience for the comfort of the summer guest," the hotel offered fireplaces in all parlours, electric bells and lights, steam and hand laundry, and "unexcelled cuisine under the immediate charge of a Boston chef." There were also log cabins to be rented by the month or season: 'The Hemlocks' had 11 rooms, 'The Firs' 5, and 'The Spruces' 7. Entertainment included a bowling alley, tennis, pool, billiards, deep sea fishing, orchestra, dancing, yachting, walking, driving, and bathing. Daily rates c. 1910 averaged $2-$5, with weekly rates set at $10-$30, depending upon the room. Advertised as only a one-night sail from Boston or a day from New York, the 'Pines' attracted 50 members of the American Medical Association Outing Club in June 1906.

PINES HOTEL

The Pines Hotel served as officers' quarters during World War I. Apparently falling upon hard financial times during the war, it went bankrupt in 1917, at which time it was purchased by Canadian Pacific Railway for $22,000, renovated extensively, and reopened in the summer of 1918.

During the late Victorian period, as urban centres grew increasingly congested and polluted, it became fashionable for the wealthy class to travel in search of health and adventure. The CPR was at the forefront of tourism development in the 1890s, promoting the myriad of tranquil and pristine opportunities afforded by a Canadian vacation, especially to the accessible and lucrative American market. The acquistion of the Digby Pines and, shortly thereafter, the Cornwallis Inn at Kentville gave the railway and steamship conglomerate a string of hotels stretching from coast to coast.

MASQUERADE BALL AT THE OLD PINES HOTEL

Dances were held at the old Pines Hotel on Tuesday, Thursday, and Saturday evenings, from 8-10 P.M. The Digby power plant normally shut down for the night around 11 P.M., but on this February evening in 1909, electric lights were kept burning at the resort until 1:30 A.M. free of charge, courtesy of plant manager A.D. Daley. The revellers photographed by Paul Yates were all said to be prominent Digby citizens and, while none were specifically identified, the following were listed among those in attendance: Mrs. G.H. Peters, Queen of Hearts; Mrs. F.W. Nichols, Fluffy Ruffles; Mrs. E. DuVernet, Hearts; Mrs. L.H. Morse, Red Cross Nurse; Miss Gertrude Oliver, Merry Widow; Nettie Dakin, Ace of Hearts; Doris Monroe, College Girl; Bessie Turnbull, Japanese Girl; Blanche Sproule, Starlight; Dr. F.E. Rice, South African Volunteer; Dr. E. DuVernet, Student; Fritz Dakin, Sailor; W.E. Tupper, Domino; L.B. Eldridge, Yachtsman; G.H. Peters, Clown; Fred A. Graham and S.E. Fuller, Quaker Twins.

NEW PINES HOTEL

Under CPR management, business was brisk at the Pines Hotel, and on May 15, 1928, work began on clearing land to build a new resort. When opened in June 1929, the Norman Chateau-style hotel and its 25 cottages could accomodate 250 guests with dining for three hundred. Daily room rates for 1936 were set at $7-$9 per person, and at $6 per person for a cottage. In 1966, Canadian National Railway sold the Pines Resort Hotel to the Province of Nova Scotia.

DIGBY GOLF LINKS 1925

The Digby Golf Club was organized on May 26, 1915, at which time a meeting was held to appoint officers and a Board of Directors. A nine-hole course was soon laid out in the western section of town on land loaned, leased, or rented to the club by a number of residents involved in its formation. The original clubhouse was a shed near the present Digby Regional High School on King Street, and the course was a par 34, of approximately 2,600 yards, with seven of its fairways crossing town streets. Before the days of wooden tees, each hole was supplied with a sandbox and water bucket; from this the golfer shaped a small mound of sand upon which the ball was placed to tee off. A "Grey Goose" golf ball—the best of its time—sold for 65 cents. Six of the Digby Golf Club's nine holes "gave one a sweeping view of the Annapolis Basin," and by June 1916 the Saint John Globe wrote of the opportunity for passengers aboard the Saint John-Digby ferry to play a round during the steamer's four-hour stopover. Green fees were $1.00, and an early "town season ticket" cost $5.00; this rose in the 1930s to $20.00 for resident members, with "summer visitors" paying $35.00. Since tourism contributed heavily to Digby's economy during summer months (cutting into residents' playing time), local hotels helped to defray the costs of course maintenance. Groundskeepers made 13 cents an hour while caddies, depending upon age and experience, were paid 15-20 cents for 9 holes, and 25-35 cents over 18 holes. When the new Pines Hotel opened an 18-hole championship course in 1931, players had the luxury of two courses until, in 1939, the Digby Golf Club closed.

A Digby baseball club was organized in 1897 in an effort to "revive interest" in local athletics. At least 30 young men signed up to play, with elected officers at the time being W.A. Morgan, President; L.H. Guptill, Vice-President; J.D. Clarke, Secretary-Treasurer; and W.A. MacLaren, Captain. A baseball diamond was laid in the south end of town on the Bacon Field bounded by Queen Street, First Avenue

(then called First Alley) and St. Mary's Street. Lacking the necessary equipment, "a complete set of apparatus" was procured from Boston. According to *Digby Courier,* the team was quite successful, especially against its chief rival in neighbouring Annapolis Royal. Interesting to note is the jargon of early sports reporting. According to an August 16, 1897 article, covering a 13-4 Digby romp over its cross-county opponent, "Arthur Murphy, the Digby twirler and Jimmy Carroll, his elegant supporter were the heroes of the hour....Fred McBride and Alex Martell, both Digby players, were applauded for the fine catches they made under difficult circumstances. Charlie Dupes, Digby's first baseman responded every time when wanted...."

Cricket and boxing were two other popular sports, with local pugilists like Kid Art, Bomber Jack, Cat Wilkins, Pigskin Melanson, Pops Saulnier, and Mexie Daley receiving considerable coverage in local sports columns of the early 1900s.

DIGBY A.A.A. HOCKEY TEAM

A 1915 photo of the Digby Amateur Athletic Association hockey team, which later was changed to the Red Ravens. Pictured in the back row (left to right) are Fred Wilson, G.F. Nason, Manager, Doug Syda; middle row: George Merkel, L. Smith, Captain Frank Anderson; front row: Gerald Syda, D. Dakin. Hockey games were played between teams from Digby, Annapolis, Bridgetown, and Church Point. As

with baseball, Digby-Annapolis games drew large crowds and were "hotly contested" affairs, both on and off the ice. The Annapolis team reportedly suited up an entire family line in the 1920s—a father and four sons. Digby at that time had a natural ice surface in the Victoria rink on Queen Street, which hosted a variety of community events. Exhibitions, hospital fairs, dances and political rallies were held in summer, with skating and games of shinny and organized hockey during winter months. C.E. Walker owned and operated the rink, which was built in 1912 and burned in February 1934. During the twenties and thirties, the Digby Ravens reached the provincial finals for seven consecutive years. A noteworthy story associated with the Central Valley Hockey League and Victoria rink happened when Digby was scheduled to host a playoff game that would determine which team would go on to the championship final. Digby's opponent complained the rink surface did not meet official measurements as to length. Not wanting to lose home-ice advantage, the Digby Hockey Association had the west end of the rink torn out. Ice blocks were cut from a nearby pond and laid in place to reach the required dimensions. After filling the cracks with water and allowing sufficient time to freeze, the game went on as scheduled.

CANNON BANKS AT LOW TIDE

With the backdrop of Beaman's Mountain in the distance, five women, possibly tourists, stroll the beach below the Cannon Banks at low tide in this late 1800s photo. Crib works like those depicted here were built at various locations along the shoreline to stem the eroding Fundy tides. A tale associated with this embankment dates to the late 1700s: a vessel arrived at Digby with seven corpses on board—five adults and two children—all having succumbed to the dreaded smallpox. Their bodies were entrusted to the Anglican Rector, Reverend Roger Viets, but at that time Digby didn't have any consecrated burial ground. Following a Christian ceremony, Reverend Viets interred the seven in his pasture near the water's edge on the Cannon Banks. Over the years, the embankment eroded to such a degree that coffins were exposed, and those of two children and one adult were washed away, never to be recovered. The Rector had new coffins built for the remaining four, and reburied them in one grave at the centre of his orchard some distance from the receding shoreline. However, by 1897 the Fundy waters had again brought the coffins to the light of day. Having heard the stories of earlier days, Viet descendents searched local records to determine the source of the grizzly find. Coming to realize "these relics of humanity were an ancient trust in the Viets family," the bones were finally laid to rest in a proper burial plot.

GUIDES OF THE NORTH WOODS

Major John Daley fishing party at Sixth Lake, Digby County, 1890s. Four Bear River Mi'kmaq guides pose beside a crude log camp: standing (L-R) are Malti Pictou, Joe Lewis; seated (L-R) John McEwan, Louis Peters. A fifth unidentified guide with hands on hips stands to the far left at rear.

As tourism developed in the late 1800s with improved steamship and railway travel, the five southwestern counties of Nova Scotia—Annapolis, Digby, Yarmouth, Shelburne, Queens—with their thousands of lakes, rivers, and streams, became popular destinations for sportsman from the eastern seaboard of the United States. Men of fame and fortune canoed and portaged the back country on trips sometimes lasting a month. However, most 'sports' were content to remain closer to civilization, forming clubs and building private lodges to which they returned year after year. John D. Rockefeller, Teddy Roosevelt, Babe Ruth, Zane Grey, and Jack Dempsey were a few of the better-known people to fish and hunt in the area. For one or two dollars a day, the services of an experienced hunting and fishing guide could be hired through many of the hotels. Bear River, Southville, and Weymouth were all popular starting points for trips into Digby County with Mi'kmaq, Blacks, Acadiens, and Anglos all offering their services as guides. Bear River was especially busy as it was "the gateway to the interior of western Nova Scotia" as well as home to a number of renowned Mi'kmaq guides. Clarke Brothers advertised its general store as the Headquarters For Sportsmen's Supplies: "Bear River and its tributaries afford the finest Trout fishing in Nova Scotia. It is also a Hunter's Paradise. Fishing and Hunting parties supplied with Guides and Outfitters at Short Notice. Birch Bark and Canvas Canoes always on hand for sale." In the 1920s it was reported that 23 Bear River guides (with parties) were seen on Ninth Lake Stream at one time.

The Good Old Days

Two portraits of a simpler time when bonds of family and community were strong. In addition to picnics and family parties, another source of popular entertainment was the "Country Round," described here by a Bear River resident in *Heritage Remembered*: "With the smaller children safely in bed, and myself settled down to

PICNIC EXCURSION FROM BEAR RIVER, 1893

do my spelling, Father and Mother would go out to see one of the neighbours in the cart. Sometimes we would have someone to visit us, and the men would talk about the weather and crops and sometimes about politics. If anyone had a newspaper, whatever its age, they would bring it to share. My mother and her visitors would go into the side room and talk about babies and cooking recipes and a lot of things I didn't understand. It made my mother very happy when we had people in on the round."

Saturday night was the highlight of the week for rural folks, as this was the time to go to town with its "village stores, the streets bustling with the horse drawn

PARTY AT SNOW'S HOME-STEAD, DIGBY

traffic and the whole families of shoppers, skilled in stretching out the value of what money they had. Ice cream and toffee apples placed within reach of small hands and a small coin by smiling storekeepers; the meetings and greetings shared after a whole week of separation; of news and views, political and personal, aired and shared with good humour and friendly argument. Then climbing sleepily into cart or sleigh to make their way home by the country roads, under the stars or in the frosty air of a winter night. It was on the main street and among people enjoying a well earned respite from the tedium of hard work and enforced isolation, that the true heart of the community beat most strongly. All this has now gone...and the community is poorer because of its loss."

Sandy Adams fishing party

An early 1900s Digby tourism brochure carried the following advertisement for Sandy Adams: "Yacht Mabel Beatrice. The undersigned is now prepared to take parties desiring a sail on the Basin or a fishing trip to any part of the Basin or Bay of Fundy. A long experience in yacht sailing and a thorough knowledge of all the fishing grounds. Terms reasonable." Digby offered ample sporting opportunities for the summer angler as attested to by this bountiful catch. There was tuna off Cape St. Mary's and salmon fishing on Salmon River at Clare, deep sea-fishing for mackerel and pollock in the Bay of Fundy or from wharves along the French Shore and Digby Neck, flounder in Digby Harbourr and runs of striped bass in the tidal waters of Bear River and Digby Joggin. In 1908 three guests of the Pines Hotel caught 850 pounds of fish in two hours.

WESTERN NOVA SCOTIA YACHT CLUB

The Annapolis Basin was popular with yachting enthusiasts and, in August 1898, the Digby Yacht Club was formed. Reports indicate the beginnings of yachting can be traced to a number of Digby residents, including Oakes Dunham, Will Hutchinson, and Joseph Millberry, who purchased shares in the *Gytha* "for their sailing pleasure." In those years Jimmie Main owned a boathouse and railway haul out at the head of the Government Wharf (seen in the background). According to Digby native Fritz Dakin, who later became Commodore of the Digby Yacht Club: "The outing of a fine summer evening was to rent a boat from Jimmie and row along the waterfront. Later he also had the yacht *Pegasus* and that was practically the beginning of the tourist business on the harbour." (Another early vessel to cater to tourists was the *John Gilpin* captained by Gus Winfield.) "Those were the days when the celebration of the year came on the first of July, Dominion Day, and the main attraction was the program of water sports, dory races, tub races, sculling races and the thrilling race of the fishing boats from the Annapolis shore. No motors in those days and the boats would line up with sails down, and when the starting gun was fired the boys would certainly scramble to get the sails up and away." In 1913, the Digby Yacht Club was reorganized into the Western Nova Scotia Yacht Club, which is still in existence today. The original registry showed 70 members, the principal officers being O.S. Dunham, Commodore; Howard Anderson, Vice-Commodore; James Cripps, Rear Commodore; P.W. Holdsworth, Secretary; Fritz Dakin, Treasurer.

BOAT SLIPS AT THE PAVILLION & BANDSTAND, C. 1910

The public boat slips featured here were located along the harbour shore, behind
the present tourist bureau. Reference has been made to one of these, belonging to
M.L. Oliver. The viewing pavillion, to the rear of which was the bandstand, offered
canteen facilities and rentals for small boats and bicycles. It was washed into the
Basin during the March storm of 1931 (described in Chapter 1). The starting point
for the early boat races was located here, later changed to the top floor of the
Central Grocery on Water Street. Captain James Wright, a "rabid fan," was official
timekeeper for the popular weekly event; Digby came to a standstill on Tuesday
afternoons when shops closed up because "almost everyone was interested in the
races." During the "big boom of 1911 and 1912" the Club House was housed in a
building later known as Sam's Clothing Store. Around 1901, Interprovincial Races
were sponsored by the Digby club featuring the local yachts *Viking*, *Canada*,
Hermes, *Regina* and *Sylvia*. The *Regina*—owned by A.J. Lutz, captained by
W.W. Hayden, and sailed by an all-Digby crew—held the trophy when the races
were discontinued.

A SUMMER CRUISE IN DIGBY HARBOUR

During World War I, and for a number of years after, the Western Nova Scotia Yacht Club was relatively inactive, although "a number of die-hards kept the sailing spirit alive." In 1938 with the Depression winding down, renewed interest in the club increased yacht numbers to 11 power launches and 20 sailing boats. Undated records indicate later developments to include 45 members, 10 sailboats and 9 power boats, with plans to build a new Club House in the south end of town on land provided by Miss Charlotte Gilpin.

DIGBY POOL HALL

John Daley operated an "oyster and billard saloon" in Digby as early as 1871, and the *Digby Courier* of Feb. 5, 1875 printed an advertisement for Harry Whyte's Billard Room on Upper Water Street, offering patrons "cigars and cordials." In 1910, the Digby Pines Hotel claimed to have the only pool and billard tables in Digby. It is apparent from this c. 1920s photo that playing pool was not a males-only game, as the lady taking her shot looks quite comfortable with a cue. A sign overhead set table rates at 40 cents per hour.

DIGBY BRASS BAND 1890S

Front Row, L-R: George Holdsworth, John McBride, Bill Holdsworth, Fred Rice, Eugene McBride, Arthur Cousins, Fulton Titus, Fred McBride; Back Row, L-R: George Peters, Will Oliver, Jim Richam, Oakes Dunham, Guy Viets, Ernest Burnham. Digby had a variety of brass, concert, and civic bands over the years. Weekly concerts at the bandstand; dances in the Pines Hotel and Victoria Rink; festive occasions such as Dominion Day, Empire Day, the Brittain Cup Races; and visits by dignitaries the likes of Sir Wildfred Laurier would all have been times when Digby bands performed. Some hotels also advertised an orchestra for the supper-hour enjoyment of patrons, the Pines, for example, having a five-piece ensemble. Photographer Paul Yates was an instrumental force in the development of music during his years at Digby. A biographical note accompanying his photo collection at the Public Archives of Nova Scotia describes Yates's chief vocation as being music: "He taught music and organized glee clubs in Digby. A renowned bandmaster, Yates directed bands in both Annapolis Royal and Digby, and at one point organ-ized a seventy-piece concert band drawing upon both communities. He was a member of the Canadian Bandmasters Association and a guest conductor on repeated occasions at concerts in Toronto and other large North American cities. John Philip Sousa and Arturo Toscannini were personal friends of Yates, the latter having given him a conductor's baton." In August 1928, the Grenadier Guards Band of Montreal came to Digby; in 1938, Chester F. Whiting, W.O., Bandmaster for the heralded 110th Cavalry Band visited Yates from Boston and guest-conducted part of the evening's concert. The band room for many years was located on the top floor of the Central Grocery on Water Street, but moved to the old Daley power plant on First Avenue in 1926.

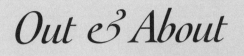

Chapter 6

Out & About

WOHNEDA LODGE, SMITH'S COVE

Smith's Cove dates to 1759, when Colonel Jonathan Hoar from Massachusetts received a land grant encompassing five thousand acres from the mouth of Bear River to a cove at the south-east section of Joggin. Joseph Potter was the first British subject to settle there in 1763, but exchanged his grant in 1783 with that of Joseph Smith, for whom the community was later named. A thriving settlement based on farming, fishing, and trade was subsequently established by Loyalist emigrants. At the turn of the 20th century, one of the principal industries was tourism, as American visitors discovered the "invigorating and healthful" climate and tranquil beauty afforded by the Cove's location along the waters of the Annapolis Basin. Hardwick House, Pleasant View House (later changed to Out-of-the-Way Inn), Harbor View Hotel, Mountain Gap, Verandah Rest and Cabins, and Bay View Farm were among the earliest tourist establishments. The first hotel was the Presto, opened c. 1880 by Benjamin Hunt. Later called the Imperial House, and changed again in 1908 to Wohneda Lodge, the "landmark of old time coaching days" burned to the ground in April 1929.

HARBOR VIEW HOTEL, SMITH'S COVE

William Cossaboom opened Harbor View Hotel c. 1900, advertising the up-scale tourist resort as "a unique and charming summer home for families of the better class." Charles F. Chase from New York was a business associate in the beginning, renting out cabins at Argonaut Knoll on Harbor View Point,while Cossaboom, who soon took over sole ownership, rented other cabins nearer the main hotel. Smith's Cove was easily accessible to the burgeoning American tourist trade of the early 1900s. Steamship service from Boston to Yarmouth (16 hours) and Saint John to Digby (3 hours) connected with Dominion Atlantic Railway trains that stopped at Imbertville Station, within 50 feet of the hotel grounds. For those arriving by way of the Flying Bluenose express train, Harbor View sent pick-up service to the Digby station for the three-mile trip to the hotel. Summer business was brisk, and by 1924 a brochure advertised an electric light plant, salt-water swimming pool, large dancing and amusement pavilion, and an Annex with "wide verandas, large airy rooms with private bath, electric lights and the comforts of home for families or individuals not requiring private cabins." Shortly after the Annex opened, fire destroyed the main hotel, including its glassed-in dining room (pictured here) which seated two hundred guests. Dining arrangements were shortly opened at the spacious Annex, and operations resumed with minimal disruption. Despite William Cossaboom's death in 1927 and a number of proprietors after, the hotel continued to flourish over the years and, while its class system of clientele may have long since changed, Harbor View today enters its second century catering to the summer tourist.

Cottage life at Harbor View

Two women enjoy a quiet rock on the verandah of Byrne's Cottage at Harbor View House and Bungalow Colony. Early brochures touted management's position that "a carefully exercised policy of soliciting only the most desirable class of patrons has resulted in an entire colony of people with whom it is a pleasure—even an honour—to associate." To this end, Harbor View's grounds had a colony of 30 cabins, some privately owned, others rented fully furnished. The popularity of cabin life necessitated rental bookings a year in advance, and those wishing to own could make arrangements with hotel management to build one "at surprisingly low cost." In addition to golf, tennis, sailing, bathing, horse-back riding, clam bakes, and dancing, a unique "out-door amusement" provided by Harbor View was its two wilderness camps at Sixth Lake in the back country of Digby County. Accessible within three hours by auto, then canoe and portage, it was said that ladies "will find life at this camp, with its home-like comforts, a novel and delightful experience." A five-day adventure for two cost $75, which included food and lodging, guides, canoe, and fishing licences. "You may leave Boston after lunch, and have your own trout for supper next evening at this camp."

The Birch Chapel of St. Anne, commonly referred to as the "Church in the Wildwood," was built by Ralph Cossitt in 1919 at Harbor View Hotel. Nestled along a wooded road on hotel land donated by proprietor William Cossaboom, its construction was supervised by Reverend John F. Richardson, Anglican Bishop from Fredericton, N.B. One of the chapel's principal benefactors was a Miss Estella

C. Ogden from New Jersey, who owned a cabin at Harbor View. In addition to monetary gifts, Miss Ogden donated all hangings, altar cloths, Fair linen, church bell, and organ. Her companion, Miss Helen Simpson, contributed the pulpit, and for many years assumed responsibility for beautifying the chapel with floral arrangements before services. Intended at the time as a house of worship primarily for the summering guests at Harbor View, the Church in the Wildwood remains a popular attraction in season today.

This unidentified early 1900s studio portrayl of an impeccably dressed woman and infant belies the daily lot faced by most Blacks at that time. History tells us that more than 3,500 free Black United Empire Loyalists earned passage to Nova Scotia between 1782-84 because of their allegiance to Britian during the American Revolutionary War. Another 1,200 or more arrived as slaves of white Loyalist

settlers. Two hundred and eleven Blacks settled in 1783 on Digby's outskirts at Brindley Town, a name later changed to Westville and now forming part of Conway. At the time, this modest number was the second largest Black population in Nova Scotia, after the 1,500 at Birchtown, near Shelburne. Sixty-nine of Digby's emigrants had served in the Black Pioneers, the only all-Black British regiment of the war. Enticed with promised land grants of five hundred to six hundred acres, a meagre 76 one-acre lots were allocated—and a number of these only after a six-year wait. Many Blacks were artisans and tradesmen whose skills were ignored by a government that saw them as "the principal source of labour and improvement" for the developing colony. Following the Sierra Leone exodus in 1792, and a tendency of those remaining to migrate to larger centres like Halifax, Brindley Town was reduced to only a quarter of its original number. Those who stayed faced decades of segregation and racial discrimination, labour exploitation, shortages of the basic life necessities, and suppressed educational opportunities. In the face of low morale and overwhelming adversity they pushed on, "striving to improve their lot, placing their reliance on God, their chosen leaders and their community orgainizations" and through their perserverance built the foundation for Digby County's Black population today. Heavyweight boxer Sam Langford (c.1884-1956) from Weymouth is perhaps the county's most recognizible Black of his time. Known in fighting circles as the "Boston Tar Baby," Langford reputedly fought more than six hundred bouts between 1902-1923. Despite losing sight in his right eye in 1917 (he was legally blind by 1924), Langford continued to fight, tracking his shadowy opponent in the ring by listening for the sound of shuffling footsteps.

BEAR RIVER MI'KMAQ, 1890S

In 1898 there were 160 Mi'kmaq in Digby County, most living on the L'sitkuk Reserve in Bear River, with six families at St. Bernard and a few others at Little River. Relegated to a life of poverty, their meagre income came from driving logs in the spring of the year, guiding sportsmen, and selling porpoise oil, deer meat, berries, baskets, axe handles, and trinkets. In this late 1890s photo two families from Bear River paddle to their summer camp near Bay View at Digby Gut to hunt porpoise. In the background is the Dominion Atlantic Railway trestle at the mouth of the river as it enters the Annapolis Basin. Archeological evidence has shown that the hillside and beach area to the left was used for Mi'kmaq summer campsites dating back two thousand years. One tradition that survived until the early 1900s was the porpoise harvest at Bay View. Two men hunting in 20-foot birchbark canoes using muzzle loaders and spears (seen here in the bow of the canoe), some-times killed as many as 12 porpoise a day in the Bay of Fundy. These would then be taken to beach camps where some of the meat would be eaten and the oil rendered by drying and boiling the blubber. Some hunters took as many as two hundred porpoise in a season; Malti Pictou, who lived to be 103 years old, is said to have once killed four hundred. Porpoise oil was prized as machine lubricant—a single porpoise producing about one and a half gallons. This proved a much needed source of income for Mi'kmaq, who bottled and marketed it locally in Digby and Saint John, New Brunswick. Among native people, porpoise oil was used for leather softener, laxative, as a remedy for ear aches, and for baiting bear traps.

"POINT PULL AND BE DAMNED"

A 1906 photo taken at Digby Gut features a Mi'kmaq summer encampment on the Digby shore near a spot called "Rattling Beach," named for the sound resulting from waves moving small stones back and forth. In the distance is the Victoria Beach side of Annapolis Basin, the point of land visible known as "Point Pull and Be Damned." Legend has it that in the days before gasoline engines, dorymen attempting to round the point and fish in the Bay of Fundy found it impossible to row against the six-knot current that rushed along there during periods of flood tide. As a consequence, several fishermen would walk the shore with a bow line over their shoulders while one man remained in the boat to navigate the rocks, a procedure repeated many times until all boats were clear of the point. These tow men came to be called 'Vulgar Boatmen,' in reference to the fact that "they didn't sing much but they sure did a heck of a lot of cussing."

Paul Yates
Rights Reserved.

Little River, N.S.

LITTLE RIVER, DIGBY NECK

Digby Neck is a narrow ribbon of land approximately 40 miles long, stretching from Digby to the "Islands"—Long Island and Briar Island. Averaging a mere two miles in width, the "Neck" is sea girthed on one shore by the Bay of Fundy, and on the other by the waters of St. Mary's Bay. The groundfish, lobster, and herring fisheries have been the life support of its 15 communities for more than two centuries. A prominant figure in Little River's fishery was Robert Austin, whose father John moved to Little River in 1887 from Smith's Cove where (as described in Chapter 2) he established Canada's first finnan haddie business. The Austins left Smith's Cove for Little River because fish were said to more plentiful on Digby Neck. By 1897, Robert Austin's processing plant employed twenty-five workers and annually produced fifty thousand tins of their famous Thistle brand finnan haddies, "well known as the superlative of excellence." Described as a "thorough business man [whose] methods and dealings are of the kind that bring success" Austin also processed canned mackerel and manufactured his own cans, "having full outfit on the premises." The Austins operated at Little River until World War I and are also credited with opening similar factories at Belliveau Cove and New Edinburgh.

SANDY COVE

A mystery surrounds Sandy Cove, as baffling today as it was 137 years ago. On an August day in 1863, notice was taken but no thought given to a rowboat making its way toward land from a vessel anchored offshore. The following morning, two farmers, drawn by the frantic screams of a boy, made a shocking discovery. On the beach above the high water mark was a man with no legs! Some biscuits and a jug of water lay within his grasp. Alive and well dressed, he was in relatively good health considering his recently amputated stumps were still bandaged and bleeding. He was carried into the village and billeted. The stranger did not, or could not, speak until his dying day, some 40 years later.

From something he mumbled when first asked his name, he was forever after known as Jerome. In due course a special government allowance of two dollars a week was alloted for his keep. It was thought Jerome may have been French or Italian and thus better served living with the Acadians at Clare, across the St. Mary's Bay. Jerome lived at Meteghan for a number of years, then moved to St. Alphonse, where he died on April 19, 1912; he was buried in the Meteghan Cemetery. Jerome reportedly learned to walk well on his stumps, and possessed amazing strength, with a violent temper to match. One source claims he did speak, but only with children, never adults. Many theories have circled about Jerome's identity, from where he came, why his legs were amputated and by whom, and how he came to be left on a beach at Sandy Cove. No one may ever know.

Leify Smith and her 30-pound Goose, c. 1912

Little is known of Leify Smith other than the fact that she and her brother Ben lived a hermit's life on Digby Neck between Sandy Cove and Centerville in the early 1900s. They were described as being a "curious family" who were suspicious of

modern medicine and conveniences, refusing on one occasion a local doctor's gift of a much-needed new stove. Leify was also very superstitious, and was said to go well out of her way on occasion to avoid crossing a wagon-wheel track in her path, choosing instead to walk to its starting point before continuing on; she felt that crossing elsewhere would surely result in bad luck.

Tiverton sits at the eastern tip of Long Island, separated from East Ferry on the mainland of Digby Neck by Petite Passage. At the west end of Long Island, 12 miles distant, is Freeport and Grand Passage, across from which lies Briar Island and the fishing village of Westport. Loyalists settled Tiverton and Freeport c. 1784-

85, although it was Champlain in 1605 who gave Long Island its name. History suggests that a Nathaniel Bates and others kept a "fishing post" at Freeport before the Loyalist arrival, as it was here the ship *Joseph* stopped in 1783 to secure a pilot to guide settlers on to Digby.

Tiverton at first was called Petite (in reference to the narrowness of the strait) but its name was changed in 1867 to honour one of its long-serving school teachers, Thomas Mildon, whose birthplace was Tiverton, England. Tiverton, Long Island was a natural site for settlement as the narrow water passage here gave fishermen a direct route between the Bay of Fundy and St. Mary's Bay. Martin Blackford operated the first ferry across Petite Passage, while George Morrell, in 1817, was the first ferryman at Grand Passage.

In 1911, Guy Morehouse from Sandy Cove was mail carrier for the Digby Neck Mail Company, which had the contract for mail delivery between Digby and the Islands. Morehouse delivered mail for 52 years, never once during that time losing a single mailbag. His route ended at East Ferry, where an exchange was made for delivery on Long and Brier Islands. Morehouse began his career on horseback, but on April 28, 1911, he became the first in Nova Scotia to carry mail using an automobile. Horses were still employed for winter travel until 1920, when Morehouse outfitted a Reo bus with a plow to keep the road open, another first for snow removal in the province. Guy Morehouse is also credited with designing and building the first snowmobile in 1920, but it's said that Virgil White from New Hampshire beat him to the patent office by a scant two weeks.

This c. 1900 photo depicts a fish plant at Freeport with haddock on rods waiting to be taken into the smoke houses for curing. In 1897, the following excerpt appeared in the *Digby Courier:*

"At Freeport there is a fleet of twelve vessels and sixty boats. The leading firm here is Hains Brothers. Milton Hains and Edwin Hains are sons of the late Bartholomew Hains, who established the business nearly sixty years ago....They

have a large patronage in their general store, where a full stock of family and fishing supplies is carried, and known as one of the most reliable retail houses in the country. Besides this, however, Hains Brothers' fishing business is a large one....They ship between 8,000 and 9,000 quintals of dry fish each year to the American and West India markets. They own five vessels and employ fifty men, beside encouraging all such labor as comes their way. The total fisheries of Freeport are placed at $141,000 and the business controlled by Hains Brothers forms a large proportion of this amount. Messrs. Hains are known as model business men, and have a reputation, local and foreign, most creditable."

Partway between Freeport and Tiverton is Long Island's only other community of Central Grove. It was here, in 1933, the *Tiny Tattler* was first printed, claimed to be the smallest weekly newspaper in the world. The thin, dime-novel-sized publication was advertised as "an independent newspaper devoted to the interests of Long and Brier Islands." Edited by Ivan Shortliffe and Rupert Cann, it was published bi-weekly from 1933-37, then weekly from 1937-43.

Joshua Slocum was born in 1844 on the Slocomb farm at Mt. Hanley, Annapolis County. (He is said to have changed the spelling of his last name in later years when he lived in the U.S.) At the age of eight, his family moved to Brier Island, his mother's home of origin, where his father began making fishermen's boots at Westport. Slocum went to sea when he was 14 and in 1895 embarked upon a three-year voyage from Boston in his 37-foot sloop *Spray* that would make him internationally famous as the first man to sail solo around the world. In 1909

Slocum—then 65—began a voyage from Martha's Vineyard off Cape Cod to South America where he intended to explore the headwaters of the Amazon River. He was never heard from again.

David Welch, a fisherman from Maine, was Brier Island's first resident, settling into a log cabin with his new bride c. 1769 to pursue the lucrative fishery. It was not until 1783, however, that an influx of 11 families of Loyalist stock permanently settled the island. In his county history, Isaiah Wilson writes of Brier Island and its only settlement: "Brier Island, four miles long, one and one-half wide, is the westernmost land belonging to Nova Scotia. Thickly settled, finely adorned, enterprising and picturesque, Westport is one of the foremost fishing stations on the western coast....Brier Island especially, from its peculiar location enjoyed but little intercourse with the County settlements on mainland until the ferry across Grand Passage (1817) was established." In 1787, Brier Island was populated by only 58 people, a number which steadily increased to 678 in 1861, and to more than 1,000 at the turn of the century. By the 1860s Westport was a flourishing community containing 120 houses, 3 churches, and a number of general stores, in addition to blacksmith shops, cooperages, hotels, fish processing plants, fertilizer factory, and a copper mine. During summer months in the early 1900s, the "invigorating climate, with its smack of fog and nearly pollen-free air" enticed many American tourists to Brier Island. Still a popular summer retreat today, Joshua Slocum dubbed it "The Island of Plenty."

Captain Ellsworth Coggins's ancestors were among the first United Empire Loyalists to settle Brier Island. Coggins left school in 1933 and signed on the three-masted schooner *Mary B. Brooks* from Weymouth. While still in his teens, Coggins shipped out as an ordinary seaman aboard the *Daniel Getson*, owned and operated by G.O. Hankinson of Weymouth. Under the command of Captain Arthur Moore from Westport, the vessel began a thousand-mile voyage south, during the course of which the mate was swept overboard, Captain Moore become gravely ill (he died just 11 days into the trip), and Coggins —not yet 20 years old—was left to sail the storm-battered ship to Turk's Island, with the help of three teenaged mates. From here Coggins wired Hankinson in Weymouth of his plight. Sources differ as to what transpired next, one reporting that Coggins was instructed to sail the ship back to Nova Scotia, another saying that a replacement skipper was sent to bring the *Getson* home. While the first makes good reading and the second would appear to be more plausible, the fact

remains that Ellsworth Coggins cut his teeth early under sail. It was the start of an illustrious career at sea; he eventually went on to serve in the Royal Canadian Navy during W.W. II, reaching the rank of Lieutenant-Commander, and to captain the replicas H.M.S. *Bounty* (pictured here at the wheel) and the *Bluenose II*. It was written in 1968 that Captain Ellsworth Coggins held the distinction of "being one of the few men of this generation who has sailed the traditional Nova Scotia course—fishing-boat, schooner, motor vessel, steamer, and back to sail with diesel auxilliary."

Isaiah Wilson writes that Acadian Pierre Doucet built the first vessel ever constructed in the county at Doucet's Point, Belliveau Cove. While not giving a
specific date, Wilson does say that Doucet, his crew, and his vessel were all lost off
Brier Island during heavy squalls in 1792. Shipbuilding was a considerably larger

industry in Digby county than it was in Digby town, with the French Shore along
St. Mary's Bay being particularly busy. Noted builders for the 1860s were Francis
Bourneuf and John W. Lovitt at Clare; Isaac H. Doane, Benjamin Killam, Ira and
Benjamin Raymond at Salmon River; William Henry Jenkins, Beaver River; James
Lovitt, St. Mary's Bay. These men made their mark in the trade, as evidenced by
Francis Bourneuf who, in 1851, built the 1,495-ton *Bourneuf* at Belliveau Cove for
Allison & Spicer of Saint John, N.B.; the three-decked vessel was the largest ever
constructed in Nova Scotia up to that time. In 1853, the 1,670 ton *Hotspur* slid
down the Bourneuf ways, the largest vessel built that year in the province. The
County of Yarmouth came out of H.P. Boudreau's yard at Belliveau Cove in 1883;
contracted for W.D. Lovitt, she was, at 2,154 tons, the second-largest wooden
vessel ever built in Nova Scotia after the famous 2,459 ton *W.D. Lawrence* from
Maitland. While Yarmouth, interestingly, was noted in the late 1800s as one of the
world's premier shipping ports, much of her fleet was constructed in Digby County
shipyards at Salmon River, Beaver River, Church Point, Gilbert's Cove, Meteghan,
Saulnierville and St. Mary's Bay.

Featured in this 1919 photo is Bernie Melanson's shipyard at Gilbert's Cove.
R.B. Powell writes in *Scrap Book Digby Town & Municipality*, "To Captain Bernie
Melanson belongs the unique experience of sharing in the shipment of the last
cargo carried by a small coastal craft from the St. Mary's Bay to New England
(lumber, 1957) and of the last shipment of a cargo (puncheon staves, 1955) from
the St. Mary's Bay to the West Indies....These two incidents completed a chapter in
the history of the St. Mary's Bay. "

TERN SCHOONER, C. 1915

Hundreds of three-masted schooners called 'terns' (from the Latin *terni* meaning "set of three") were built in the Maritime provinces from the 1870s to 1920. In *Sails of the Maritimes* author John P. Parker identifies more than 70 as being built in Digby County. Comeauville, Weymouth, Meteghan River, Belliveau Cove, Meteghan, Salmon River, Church Point, Grosse Cocques, Gilbert's Cove, Bear River, and Little Brook all built these versatile vessels. Tern schooners varied greatly in size—from 21 tons to 640 tons, most averaging two hundred to three hundred tons. They were popular in the coastal trade, generally requiring a crew of only six men or less, which minimized costs. According to John Parker, the first tern was built in the United States in 1849, while the first Canadian three-master, the 143 ton *Zebra*, came ten years later at LaHave, N.S. Canada's second tern, the *A.F. Randolph* (155 tons) was New Brunswick-built in 1865 but owned by W.C. Warren of Digby. Meteghan River, Digby County is credited with constructing the sixth largest three-master ever, the 595-ton *Celeste D* in 1919, and the second smallest tern schooner in 1903, the 31-ton *Souvenir*. In 1918, the French Shore of Clare had 12-14 shipyards, making it "the leading wooden ship building centre in western Nova Scotia." Digby County shipyards at that time were said to employ five hundred to six hundred men, with average weekly wages totalling more than ten thousand dollars.

ELECTRIC CITY

In 1896, aristocrat Emile Charles Adolphe Stehelin moved his family from France to the backwoods of Digby County. Long bitter over the annexation of his home province following the 1870 Franco-Prussian War, the "Old Gentleman" as he came to be known, looked to build a new life for himself, wife Marie Thérèse, and their eight sons and three daughters. His son, Jean Jacques, had laid the groundwork in 1892 when he arrived in the Acadien community of Church Point in search of adventure and "a niche in the world for himself." After two years learning local ways and customs, he decided on lumbering and, with his father's financial backing, began work on a sawmill settlement 17 miles from the shipping port of Weymouth. The Stehelin wilderness empire, known as "New France," was built on the Silver River between Little Tusket and Langford Lakes. Included were a stationary mill (pictured here), tea house, club house, cookhouse, ice house, forge, office, main residence or the 'Big House,' a smaller residence, chapel, barn, recreational centre, ten thousand acres of woodland, portable mills, and a sixteen-mile railway. When an electrical generating plant was installed in 1895 to run the mill—and the three hundred lightbulbs throughout the grounds—New France came to be referred to as "Electric City." This was quite a feat for the times, considering Weymouth didn't get electricity until 1926. Blacks, Acadiens, Mi'kmaq, and Anglos all found employment with the Stehelins. Emile raised the hackles of local businessmen by paying his workers wages rather than subscribing to the traditional barter system. Times were good until the death of wife Marie Thérèse in 1910, after which Electric City was abandoned. Emile and four sons moved to Weymouth to run the firm of E. Stehelin & Company, which operated until shortly after World War I. In 1914, seven of the eight Stehelin boys marched off to war, with all surviving the conflict. Not so with their father Emile, who passed away in August 1918. After many years the New France story was revived in 1983 by grandson Paul H. Stehelin's book *Electric City: The Stehelins of New France*. In the late 1990s, what physical traces remain were placed under the auspices of the J.D. Irving Limited Unique Areas Program of Historic Site Protection.

Weymouth, N.S., from West Side

WEYMOUTH

Of the 1,144 water and steam powered sawmills in Nova Scotia in 1871, Digby County had 109—the third largest number in the province. Weymouth was considered "the lumbering centre of the county." The Sissiboo River, which runs through the town, allowed vessels to navigate two miles inland from its mouth, "forming a good and inviting harbour." Originating from a chain of lakes near the Annapolis County line 20 miles distant, the Sissiboo provided access to rich timber resources from the interior and ample water power to run sawmills. Shipbuilding was another important Weymouth industry; Colonels James Moody and John Taylor built the first vessel at Weymouth c. 1793, which completed its maiden voyage to Liverpool, England in 18 days. By 1879, 11 barques, 2 brigantines, and 4 schooners were locally owned and registered in Weymouth. In addition to foreign markets, a brisk local trade and packet ferry service developed early between Weymouth and the people of Digby Neck and Islands. It was more convenient to cross St. Mary's Bay and do business in Weymouth or nearby Meteghan than it was to endure a two-day wagon ride to Digby. Historian Isaiah Wilson writes that nineteenth century Weymouth was "one of the most prosperous and important inland Ports in Western Nova Scotia....The very extensive and numerous Mercantile Establishments, wholesale and retail, combined with the shipping interests, are incalcuble blessing to the surrounding country." However, in October 1929, Weymouth was struck a severe economic blow from which it never fully recovered. Twenty-five stores, factories and dwellings were lost in a blazing inferno, which was kept from burning the entire town only by dynamiting buildings at both ends of the main street. Damage was placed at $250,000 with only $20,000 in losses covered by insurance.

View of Weymouth, N.S., from Railway Station

WEYMOUTH

Colin Campbell was one of Weymouth's more prominent businessmen, owning seven ships in 1879. He started as a general merchant and ship owner in 1848, then opened his own shipyard in 1867 to build vessels for an extensive lumber export trade. His son George Douglas Campbell expanded the family business when he began operating a sawmill. In 1896, the Stehelin family bought out the lumber yards of G.D. Campbell, along with most of the wharves and buildings along the south side of the Sissiboo River. From 1897-1907, the Stehelin's annually shipped a million feet of lumber to South America and five hundred thousand feet of deals (three-inch thick planks of varying widths and lengths) to England. George Hankinson was another well known Weymouth merchant in the early 1900s, running a large wholesale and retail provision business as well as dealing in flour and feed. He owned three stores, and the top floor of one store housed Weymouth's only moving-picture hall. Hankinson also sold hard and soft coal from a wharf in town and was president of Hankinson Shipping Company in nearby Belliveau Cove which owned two vessels employed in carrying 1,000,000 feet of lumber annually from his mill to markets in the United States and West Indies. As demand for pulp and pulpwood grew, S. Fawes Smith, a summer tourist from Philadelphia, formed the Sissiboo Falls Paper Company in 1894 and built a pulp mill eight miles upriver from Weymouth. In 1899, Charles Burrill—a Weymouth lumber exporter—bought the Sissiboo Pulp & Paper Company and opened a second mill at Weymouth Falls. In 1904, the pulpmills and woodlands were purchased by G.D. Campbell & Company. The Quebec based St. Croix Pulp & Paper Company bought out Campbell's in 1941, along with 67,000 acres in Digby and Yarmouth Counties, and shipped pulpwood to Quebec by railway from Weymouth. At the end of World War II, St. Croix Pulp & Paper Company woodland holdings were taken over by the Mersey Paper Company which, in recent years, sold hundreds of thousands of acres to J.D. Irving from Saint John, N.B.

CLARKE BROTHERS' LUMBER WHARVES, BEAR RIVER

Bear River is unique in that its river divides the village between the counties of Digby and Annapolis. In the late 1800s, Bear River was Digby County's most thriving community. Led by Clarke Brothers, "one of the first and most enterprising business houses in the Province" the village economy was based predominately upon lumbering, shipbuilding, and trade. Bear River of the 1890s exported 10 million board feet of lumber and various wood products annually to Boston, New York, and Cuba; Clarke Brothers alone accounted for 6 million of this. Butter, eggs, apples, and cherries formed the basis of Bear River's agricultural shipments to Saint John and the United States. In addition to numerous general stores, speciality shops, woodworking factories, and craftsmen, Bear River also had its own electric power plant, telegraph office, newspaper, steamship company, and customs house. Wallace and Willard Clarke began their partnership of Clarke Brothers in 1880, and by 1918 the firm was doing three hundred thousand dollars worth of business a year and paying thirty thousand dollars in wages. Clarke Brothers' diverse ventures included a dry goods, groceries and general merchandise store, outfitters for hunting and fishing parties, ownership of the three-masted schooner Ethel Clarke, controlling shares in the Bear River Steamship Company, and acting as agents for several British and American insurance firms. Clarke Brothers owned eighteen thousand acres of woodland and a large milling operation nine miles from Bear River, at Lake Jolly. Two hundred people lived at Lake Jolly which had a saw mill, planing mill, sash and door factory, stave mill, dowel, and clothes-pin factory. The mill burned in 1923, and when a Clarke Brothers plan to build and operate a pulp mill in the 1920s at the mouth of the Bear River failed, the firm and many local investors were driven into bankruptcy.

BEAR RIVER SHIPYARDS, 1890

In the 1870s and 1880s Bear River had five shipyards turning out barques, barquentines, brigantines, and schooners. Featured here c. 1890 is John Benson's shipyard (foreground) with Tom Rice's yard in the distance near the bridge. Both were on the Digby County side of the river. Frederick William Wallace writes in his book *Wooden Ships & Iron Men* that Alpheus Marshall built and operated ships at Bear River in the 1860s, one being the 596-ton *Hattie M.* he constructed in 1869 for personal interests. Marshall followed this in 1872 with the 922-ton *Alpheus Marshall*, the largest built up to that time in Bear River. Another of 1,096 tons was contracted in 1881 for the Troops family in Saint John, N.B. Christopher Benson was Marshall's master-ship builder. When Benson passed away, his son Captain John M. Benson became yard superintendent. F.W. Wallace credits John Benson with building some of Nova Scotia's finest vessels. When the era of wooden ship-building declined in the late 1800s, Benson left Alpheus Marshall's yard and moved to Meteghan, Digby County, where he purchased a marine slip and repair yard. There he became inspector of wooden vessels in western Nova Scotia for the American Bureau of Shipping until the close of World War I. John Benson passed away in 1921 at the age of eighty-four.

BEAR RIVER CHERRY FESTIVAL

The Bear River Cherry Festival, still a popular summer attraction, was organized in 1893 by local barber George Brooks. A.B. Marshall, then one of the town's prominent citizens, remembered the gala event as something "we never thought so much about what we were going to get out of it, but about doing our best to have a good

time for the day." This c. 1920 photo shows some of the five thousand spectators who annually gathered along the river front for the traditional water sports involving the grease pole walk, swimming races, and canoeing events. Marching bands, floats, land sports, and, of course, booths selling cherries—set amid a street scene of banners, flags and bunting—were all part of the day's festivities. George Sutherland is credited with introducing cherry trees to Bear River and the surrounding countryside in the 1780s, where they flourished until devastated by an early 1920s blight, which also destroyed the village's productive apple industry. Bear River cherry trees were said to be unique in that they could regenerate from seed rather than the normal grafting method. Most orchards had 12-20 trees from which a thousand picked boxes returned $30 when shipped to Halifax, Saint John, and Boston. In addition to its cherry festival, Bear River in early years also held a "Cherry Sunday" around July 20, when crowds came to "rent" or "buy" a tree of cherries from orchard owners. Paying 50 cents to $3.00, a family or group were then allowed to pick the tree clean. American tourists were particularly smitten by the local fruit, as evidenced by this somewhat-exaggerated descriptive postcard sent to Maine:

> JULY 29, 1912. *Dear Gertrude: ....This region is beyond description for fertility and beauty. I wish you might see the orchards. Just think of 20,000 trees in an orchard. Cherries!! I ate a qt. just before going to bed the other day. Love to all.   Alice*

Four year old Maud Dowley poses with her ten-year-old brother, Charles, in what is thought to be the earliest photo of the internationally-acclaimed folk artist. Maud was born on March 7, 1903 in South Ohio, Yarmouth County, as the only daughter of Agnes and John Dowley. In 1914 the family moved to Yarmouth town.

Birth defects left Maud with sloped shoulders and her chin resting on her chest—features not apparent in this studio portrayal but which led to much ridicule and teasing from her peers. Fortu-nately Maud grew up in a nurturing environment "filled with loving parents, pets, music and painting." Her father's prosperous harness making and blacksmith business provided the means to purchase a piano and phonograph. Mother Agnes instilled an appreciation for music in her children at an early age and instructed Maud in her first art lessons, teaching her to paint watercolour Christmas cards. Following the death of her parents in the 1930s, Maud moved to Digby and lived with her Aunt Ida. On January 16, 1938 Maud married Everett Lewis, a fish peddler who owned a tiny one-room house (12 1/2 feet by 13 1/2 feet) on the Marshalltown road, next door to the poorhouse. It was here that Maud spent her remaining 32 years, living a simple, impoverished, but seemingly happy life. Despite the crippling effects of rheumatoid arthritis on her hands, Maud painted scenes of Digby County, her intent being "to entertain, to brighten people's lives with heart warming colours and subtle contradictions." On a good day she completed two paintings, using marine paints, particleboard, crude brushes, and sardine tin palettes. Maud's renditions of three-legged cows, oxen with eye lashes, driverless horse drawn sleighs, and trees out of season sold briskly from her brightly-muraled roadside home. Maud Lewis died in 1970 at the age of sixty-seven. Her Marshalltown home has been preserved in the Art Gallery of Nova Scotia, and several books, a play, a film documentary, and a travelling exhibit commemorate her life. Two-dollar paintings rendered by a woman who never travelled more than an hour's drive from her place of birth, nor considered herself an artist, now command prices in excess of one thousand times their original value.

Sources

BOOKS:

Bauld, Florence L. *Bear River—Untapped Roots.* Halifax: Minuteman Press. 1997.

Calnek, W.A. *History of the County of Annapolis.* Toronto: William Briggs. 1897.

Clayton, Hazel Maud. *Smith's Cove and Her Neighbours, Part 1.* Digby: Wallis Print, 1961.

———. *Smith's Cove and Her Neighbours, Part 2.* Digby: Wallis Print, 1968.

Davis, Anthony. *Dire Straits.* Saint John's: Institute of Social & Economic Research, Memorial University, 1991.

Erjavec, Barbara. *The Wit & Wisdom of Joe Casey.* Hantsport: Lancelot Press, 1994.

Hall, E. Foster. *Heritage Remembered.* Bear River: Bear River New Horizons Centre, 1981.

Hart, E.J. *The Selling of Canada: The CPR and the Beginnings of Canadian Tourism.* Banff, Alberta: Altitude Publishing, 1983.

Hill, Allan Massie. *Some Chapters in the History of Digby County and Its Early Settlers.* Smith's Cove, N.S.: Longview Press, 1901.

Hornsby, Stephen J. *Time & Tide: The Transformation of Bear River, N.S.* Orono, Maine: University of Maine Folklife Center, 1996.

Hutchins, Nancy Bowden. *Digby Golf Club History.* Digby: self-published, 1979.

Johnson, Ralph S. *Forests of Nova Scotia.* Halifax: Department of Lands & Forests, 1986

MacMillan, Gail. *A Breed Apart.* Halifax: Nimbus Publishing, 1998.

Mair, Nathan H. *Grace Through the Years.* Digby: self-published, 1987.

Mosher, Edith. *Old Time Travel in Nova Scotia.* Hantsport, N.S.: Lancelot Press, 1984.

Ness, Gary W. *Canadian Pacific's DAR Vol. I.* Calgary: British Railway Modellers of North America (date unknown).

Pachai, Bridglal. *Blacks.* Tantallon, N.S.: Four East Publications, 1987.

Parette, Henri-Dominique. *Acadians.* Tantallon, N.S.: Four East Publications, 1991.

Parker, Mike. *Guides of the North Woods: Hunting & Fishing Tales from Nova Scotia 1860-1960.* Halifax: Nimbus Publishing, 1990.

———. *Wood Chips & Beans: Life in the Early Lumber Woods of Nova Scotia.* Halifax: Nimbus Publishing, 1992.

———. *Where Moose & Trout Abound.* Halifax: Nimbus Publishing, 1995.

Parker, John P. *Sails of the Maritimes.* Great Britain: Hazel, Watson & Viney, 1960.

Powell, R. Baden. "Scrap Book: Digby Town and Municipality." Digby: Wallis Print, 1968.

———. "Second Scrap Book: Digby Town And Municipality." Digby: Wallis Print, 1973.

Ricker, Darlene A. *L'sitkuk*. Lockeport, N.S.: Roseway Publishing, 1997.

Robertson, Barbara R. *Sawpower*. Halifax: Nimbus Publishing. & Nova Scotia Museum, 1986

Senior Scribes of Nova Scotia. *Poverty, Poor Houses and Private Philantthropy*. Halifax: Queen's Printer, 1996.

Shea, Phil. *Brier Island*. Hantsport, N.S.: Lancelot Press, 1990.

Snow, Vincent G. *A Treasury of Digby Memories*. Self-published, 1996.

Spicer, Stanley. *Masters of Sail*. Halifax: Petheric Pres,. 1968.

Stehelin, Paul H. *The Electric City*. Hantsport, N.S.: Lancelot Press, 1983.

Stephens, David. *Iron Roads, Railways of N.S.* Windsor, N.S.: Lancelot Press, 1972.

Wade, Lennie D. *Historic Glimpses of Picturesque Bear River*. 1908

Wallace, Frederick William, *Roving Fisherman*. Gardenvale, Que.: Harpell's Press Co-operative, 1955

———— . *Wooden Ships & Iron Men*. London: White Lion Publisher, 1973.

Woods, Shirley. *Cinders & Saltwater*. Halifax: Nimbus Publishing, 1992.

Woodworth, Marguerite. *History of the Dominion Atlantic Railway*. Kentville, N.S.: Kentville Publishing Company, 1936.

Woolaver, Lance & Brooks, Bob. *The Illuminated Life of Maud Lewis*. Halifax: Nimbus Publishing, 1995.

Wilson, Isaiah W. *A Geography & History of the County of Digby*. Halifax: Holloway Brothers, 1900.

NEWSPAPERS, PUBLICATIONS & ASSORTED PAPERS:

Canadian Fisherman. August 1914. Lunenburg: Fisheries Museum of the Atlantic.

Diary of Jessie Turnbull (nee Titus). Archer Turnbull, Smith's Cove, N.S.

Digby Courier. Assorted issues from the 1890s-1930s. Halifax: Public Archives of Nova Scotia.

Historic Walking Tour Of Digby. Admiral Digby Museum. 1999.

Scrapbooks of assorted newspaper clippings. Archer Turnbull, Smith's Cove, N.S.

Shunpiking, Nova Scotia's Discovery Magazine. February/March 2000.

Writings of Judge Victor Cardoza. Admiral Digby Museum. Digby, N.S.

PUBLIC ARCHIVES OF NOVA SCOTIA:

Cardoza, Victor. "Short History of Trinity Anglican Church."

DAR "New Pines Hotel" (1929).

Digby & Digby County "Summer Play Place of N.S" (1918).

"Digby, N.S.: Diamond Anniversary Booklet" (1890-1950).

"Digby: the Delightful Restful Summer Resort" (c. 1920).

"Lour Lodge & Cottages, Digby" (1911).

"Myrtle House: Old English Inn" (1891).

Padley, Taunya J. "Church of England's Role in Settling Digby." Thesis.

Research Bulletin: "Prince Regent's Battery & Queen's Battery."

"Souvenir Album of Annapolis & Digby" (1895).

"Souvenir Booklet of Opening St. Patrick Church, Digby" (1941).

"The Pines: Acadia, the land of the happy" (1910).